Stolen Halos

Jamie Cantrell

JAMIE CANTRELL

Stolen Halos

HELP FOR HURTING WOMEN

TATE PUBLISHING
AND ENTERPRISES, LLC

This book is designed to provide accurate and authoritative information with regard to the subject matter covered. This information is given with the understanding that neither the author nor Tate Publishing, LLC is engaged in rendering legal, professional advice. Since the details of your situation are fact dependent, you should additionally seek the services of a competent professional.

The opinions expressed by the author are not necessarily those of Tate Publishing, LLC.

Published by Tate Publishing & Enterprises, LLC
127 E. Trade Center Terrace | Mustang, Oklahoma 73064 USA
1.888.361.9473 | www.tatepublishing.com

Tate Publishing is committed to excellence in the publishing industry. The company reflects the philosophy established by the founders, based on Psalm 68:11,
"The Lord gave the word and great was the company of those who published it."

Book design copyright © 2016 by Tate Publishing, LLC. All rights reserved.
Cover design by Dante Rey Redido
Interior design by Caypeeline Casas
Photography by Laurie Myers

Published in the United States of America

ISBN: 978-1-68352-262-1
1. Religion / Christian Life / Personal Growth
2. Religion / Christian Life / Inspirational
16.06.13

To all the women who have ever been broken.
May the stones thrown at you become a
firm foundation of strength and courage.

CONTENTS

Preface: Broken Ranger 9

1 Crowns and Halos 15

2 Thieves in Our Midst 29

3 I Can Do It by Myself 47

4 Search and Seizure 59

5 Grabbing Hold of Your Halo 75

6 Who Holds Your Halo 95

7 Wear It Well 113

PREFACE

Broken Ranger

"Mommy, Mommy, help," cried my six-year-old little boy as he rushed into the kitchen.

"What's wrong, honey?" I asked.

With the sound of sobbing utterances as a reply, I managed to make out two words: "He's broken." As I looked down into his tiny hand, I noticed a broken action figure. It was a green Power Ranger with a severed arm. "Can you fix him?" responded my hurt but hopeful little man with big, questioning eyes and a dirty tear-streaked face.

Assessing the damage, I picked up the pieces of broken plastic and asked, "How did he break?"

"I was smashing him with rocks," he replied with a tone that held no remorse or comprehension his actions were wrong.

"Well, baby, you can't be mean to your toys and expect them not to break. I don't know if I can fix him."

As my words sunk into his innocent mind, I saw his expression change from one of hopefulness to one of despair. His little

9

head dropped, and his little fists came up to meet his tear-filled eyes. A loud "waaahhh!" echoed through the small kitchen.

As with most mothers, my heart twisted at that sound. Desperate to do anything to stop the incessant crying, I made the one comment that puts Mommies at the top of the superhero list: "I'll fix it."

Almost immediately, the sobs ceased, and his smudged face looked at me with awe as he said, "Thanks, Mom," and bounded out of the room.

Taking a deep breath, I glanced around the tiny kitchen. The dirty dishes would have to be put on hold. The linoleum floor, with its curled-up edges, would have to wait to be swept. I had tried desperately to transform this makeshift place into a home for a little while until the kids and I could move. I had painted the kitchen a sunny, warm yellow and made homemade sunflower print curtains that adorned windows that were painted shut. The back door dragged on the floor if you tried to open it, and none of the cabinet drawers would open without using two hands and a lot of wiggling. But all of these repairs and cleaning tasks would have to wait until the little green action figure could be mended. Grabbing some super glue and various types of tape, I cleared off the only section of countertop as a work space. Laying the broken ranger onto a raggedy dish towel, I began the near-impossible task. I was feeling especially low that day. As with most women going through a divorce, some days you feel like a strong tower and other days like a blown-out tire. This was definitely a "blown tire" kind of day. As I picked up the little green arm and squeezed a dab of superglue onto ranger's socket, I heard the inner voice that speaks so often to me. It whispered, "Who puts Mommy back together when she's broken?" *Being in a fragile state of mind already, this was the opening for the floodgate of tears. How true, I thought. Through blurred vision and drops of tears on the ranger project, I continued to work diligently. This toy was not his favorite, and I could easily tell him it was broken for good. He would probably forget all about it in an hour or so. I could even go buy another. They were only a few dollars. But it was the point of the matter. Perhaps I needed to prove to myself nothing was beyond repair. I felt sort of a bond to this little trooper who had been so mistreated.*

After only a couple of minutes, my son bounced back into the room and asked if his toy was fixed yet. Not wanting him to see me crying, I kept my head down and mustered a normal sounding voice, "Not yet, honey. It's going to take a while to fix him, why don't you go back outside and play?" As I heard the sound of retreating steps and the bang of the screen door, the little voice spoke again and said, "How long will it take to fix you?" *As even more tears flowed down my cheeks, I didn't have the answer. I had no idea how long it would take to feel happy again, much less to feel normal. After some time of intricate repair tactics, I managed to get the green ranger back in one piece. Needing to let the glue dry, I left him untouched on the dishtowel and turned to the task of washing dishes and laying them on the table to dry. Once again, my disheveled, yet joyful,*

11

little boy rushed into the house and exploded through the kitchen doorway. "Look what I found," he exclaimed as he held up a stick that resembled a gun and began shooting imaginary bullets all around my kitchen. As his toy gun aimed at the counter, he spotted the green ranger, dropped his stick on the floor, and reached for his play toy. "Hey, you fixed him."

With a gasp, I hollered, "No!" and stopped his hands. "He's not ready yet. We have to let the glue dry. You can't play with him right now, and when he is ready you have to be really careful because he's not put back together real good, and he might break again," I explained, in language I hoped he would understand.

"Oh," he responded, and without another word, picked up his imaginary revolver and hopped out of the room and back outside. How ironic, I thought. To everyone else, I might seem like I'm put back together and as strong as ever, but in all reality, I'm like the broken ranger. I'm not put back together real well and very scared I might break again. With tears on the horizon once more, I laid down my dishrag, turned away from the sink, still full of soaking plates, and walked out of the kitchen into the tiny bathroom. I shut the door and had a very long and very silent cry.

❦

While this day was one of the worst during that time of my life, it was also one of my most enlightening. It was on this day I realized nothing is beyond repair. I had been living in a tiny rental house with so many holes, creaks, and cracks that slugs, spiders, and mice seemed to be constant living companions. My husband and I had recently divorced, and I was struggling not only with finances but with emotional trauma as well. Never in my life would I have thought I would be in this situation. I had the perfect marriage, the perfect partner, the perfect kids and the perfect house—until the day my husband announced his adulterous life-style. I felt very much like my son's broken ranger. Perhaps you too have experienced the smashing rocks thrown by the hand of a careless man and have found yourself to be the ranger in harm's way.

While many people can become a target or victim of hurt, women seem to be the most vulnerable. The unique traits and mothering nature of women make the hits more difficult to overcome. More often than not, women are the fixers, the caregivers, the menders, the encouragers, and the peacemakers. We hold the sticky hands of our children and kiss their dirty faces without hesitation. We take an army of little league ball players to practice and home again. We turn the dirty socks right side out prior to washing. We can twirl our little girls around like a princess and catch bugs with our boys. We make sure our children have that Halloween costume that originated totally out of their head, even if we have to make it out of scrap aluminum. We stay up all night with a sick child and chaperone wild slumber parties as well. We laugh at their jokes, discipline their misbehavior, and pray continually. Mothers are the pillar of strength for their children. They are troopers, angels, and protectors. They are cooks, chefs, and chauffeurs. But what happens when a mother is a broken ranger?

Sometimes, like the injured action figure, women may find themselves torn apart and wonder what transpired. More often than not the affliction is caused by a man who supposedly cared. The smashing hits of the rock could be anything from hurtful words, adultery, pornography, molestation, abuse, or simply being ignored and taken advantage of. Perhaps you've experienced a blow or two or three from someone you trusted, and the result was a broken ranger. All too often these hits leave women unable to mend. When a woman is in pieces, who is there to pick her up, hold her hand, kiss the boo-boos, put her back together, and watch over her until everything is all right? Unfortunately, many women can't find a repair person, so they end up mending the hurts by themselves. Sometimes these patch jobs are faulty, and as a result the world is full of women who continue to fall apart time and time again.

1

Crowns and Halos

"I want to be a princess forever, but my bubba told me when I get bigger, I can't be a princess," my four-year-old niece said. Her soft brown eyes looked terribly sad as she told me about the conversation she had with her big brother. My niece loves anything princess. She has every princess movie ever made. Her fifth birthday looked like a fairy tale, with pink fluffy dresses and jeweled crowns. The thought she might have to give up her crown someday made her terribly sad.

"Oh, you'll always be a princess in God's eyes," I told her. Then I thought about how true that statement actually is. I believe every little girl goes through a princess time of life—a time where she dreams of a perfect future with herself as center stage. The scenery in her mind is filled with fragrant flowers, make-believe animals, splendid castles, and a charming prince. And best of all, she sees herself as the princess, with a swirly gown and a glistening tiara while, in reality, most young ladies will never sit on a throne crowned with rubies and sapphires; they have all been given a sparkling halo. Every single child of the Most High has been given a special place in the heart and kingdom of God. Children are so precious to God that Jesus himself allowed the children to gather around and treated them with respect, kindness, and love. In other words, he has given every child a halo. A halo is a symbol of righteousness, purity, holiness, and glorious beauty. It is an aura of hope and wondrous expectation. It is self-respect and confidence. Little ones come into this world with this special package. They enter with a heart of innocence untainted by bitterness, anger, distrust, unforgiveness, and sin. They are trusting, sweet, loveable, and good. They care, sing, dance, and laugh without reserve. They are full of faith, life, and love. God has given little girls a special halo that is complex and diverse. It is an imbedded character of humbleness, caring, and nurturing—all the things we need in mothers. Yet he has also given them a character of courage, determination, and a fighting spirit—also things a mother needs. It is quite the perfect package of worth, dignity, eloquence, assertiveness, faith, love, guts, and grit. Little girls dream big dreams and hope high hopes. They can be anything, from a firefighter or teacher to a superhero or princess. They have their whole lives ahead of them and eagerly await their future with joyful expectations. In other words, they wear their halo well.

Stolen Halos

God desires his children to always wear their halo as splendidly as any glorious angel. As Christians, we are to be light and salt to the world. We are to be those who are full of faith and joy. But what happens when our halo gets stolen? There are people in the world who either knowingly or not steal another's glory. Either male or female can be the thief, and either one can be the victim as well. Some people manage to hold on to their halo for many years, and some find theirs ruthlessly taken at a very young age. While I'm very aware of all the different types of victims and perpetrators and in no way mean to sound biased, I'll be focusing on victimized women with men as the burglar.

Halos can be taken in all sorts of ways. Molestation, rape, verbal and physical abuse, pornography, and adultery are all ways in which women are victimized. When a man harms a woman through any of these means, he steals her halo, something God intended her to wear forever. Her identity, dreams, hopes, visions, goals, joy, and purpose can all be stripped away by one act of harm. Some actions are intentional, and others are simply done out of carelessness. Either way the injury remains the same. A husband may have a weak moment and cheat on his spouse, or he may actively seek an adulterous affair. While the intent may be different, the result is the same. A breach of trust occurred, no matter how innocent or accidental the man thought it to be. When someone hurts someone else, the intention is of little consequence. It doesn't matter how the man intended it; what matters is how the woman took it. She ends up a broken ranger or an angel without her halo.

My Halo Story

We all have a story to tell. Some may be more shocking than others. Some people have gone through things that make your heartache look like a walk in the park. However, your story is just as valid and can leave just as many scars. My story is in no way a horrific tragedy. Compared to the scars others may carry, mine are like scratches. But it is a story worth telling, and maybe someone out there can identify with it. It is a story of halos being stolen over and over again.

How young can you be to have your halo stolen? Well, there is no magical age. I guess mine was stolen around the innocent age of one, but I never knew it. My father walked out on my mother, brother, and me when I was barely walking. Apparently, adultery can be so enticing you forget you have children. My father chose to have another woman in his life and left my mom to support the two of us. She moved us to her little hometown where she was raised. We lived in a tiny house with a bathroom you could hardly turn around in. We grew up riding bikes around all the side streets, playing in the neighbors yards, and eating TV dinners while watching one of the only two channels we got reception on. We didn't have a lot, but when you don't know any different, you think you live in a mansion. I had a wonderful childhood. My mom was the best mom in the whole world. She was a first-grade teacher, which made her pretty good with my brother and me. She taught during the day and worked at my grandpa's little country general store on evenings and weekends to help support us. I remember growing up wondering a lot about my dad and why I never saw him. Mom said it was because if he saw us, he would realize how much he lost, and he just couldn't bear it. I know, now, that was a lie, but at the time the answer made us feel we had great worth. I began noticing my halo was missing when I would send pictures to my dad through my paternal grandparents, which we kept in touch with every so often. I would sign the back of my school pictures with my name and grade and sign "Love, Jamie." He never responded. Not one note or call ever came. Relatives would say I looked just like my dad. How would I know? The thought that my dad could toss me aside so easily was heartbreaking. I felt like a gum wrapper someone might toss out the window as they sped down the highway of life.

Skipping forward a few years, I regained my strength and self-worth and found my halo again. Then, on a sunny Saturday, a tragedy hit. Five of my friends were killed in a terrible car accident. One of them was my boyfriend. While this incident wasn't a deliberate halo theft, it did leave an empty hole for years to come. I was so desperate to make sense out of this senseless tragedy, I ran into the arms of anybody willing to extend them. That summer was a wild and crazy summer with parties every night and an "I don't care" attitude. I accepted a date invitation from a guy I had a crush on for quite some time. He was a few years older than me and quite a handsome young country boy. I don't even remember where we went earlier that evening; I only remember where we ended up. He said he wanted to take me to a place down by the river and show me the beautiful scenery. Looking back, how naïve could I have been? A parked car, on a river bank, with no one around for miles was the perfect location for what he had in mind. Without going into details, I was date raped. That term wasn't invented then, so there was no way to put a label on it. It was the first time I had ever been sexually active. I was lost, confused, and scarred. I remember thinking, *Oh, God, I hope no one finds out. I just want to go home.* Of course, afterward, he made the excuse that he just couldn't help himself and confessed his undying love for me. He never contacted me again. I found out later he left for the military the very next day. He knew exactly what he was doing. He wanted to have a night to remember while he spent long, lonely nights in boot camp. Unfortunately, it was a night I will never forget either. And just like that, the halo was, once again, nowhere in sight.

So, I did the only thing I knew to do. Run to someone else—anyone else—who promised an escape. This time, it was a young man who was charming, good-looking, and came from a highly religious family. His dad was even a preacher. This was it, my safety net. He would be my fortress and stronghold against the winds that seemed to blow me down. I was eighteen when I married him, and my veil attached to my tiara crown looked very much like a sparkling rhinestone halo. It wouldn't last long, though. The first punch came only a few weeks later. We were only married one year, but the emotional and physical abuse progressed rapidly. By the time the year was over, I had been hit, had my hair pulled, slapped, sexually abused, choked, kicked, cut, locked in, locked out, stranded, and become the object of target practice for the many items thrown around the house. The last straw came as I tried to leave and found a loaded shotgun aimed at my head as he dragged me into an empty bedroom. By the grace of God, I escaped and ran home to Mommy. The halo, however, didn't make it home with me.

After that, I decided enough was enough; time for me to live my life my way. I was nineteen when I went to college, but I felt like I'd already lived three lifetimes. You wouldn't have found a tougher cookie than me. I must have dated twenty guys or more during those four years. "Date them, use them, drop them, and find another" was my motto. No man would hurt me again. I would hurt them before they got the chance. Life through college was twofold. I would be in youth group on Thursday night and the bar on Friday. I held on to God with one hand but danced with the devil when I thought God wasn't looking. Finally, my halo was back. It was a little crooked, dinged up, and not nearly as shiny as it should have been, but I wore it the best I could. Then, out of the blue, an unsuspecting thief approached. Being a freshman at college and new to a big city, I was way too trusting. I found everything terribly exciting, but not terribly dangerous. That was my first mistake. It was a cool November night, and I was walking from my dorm to the parking lot where I parked my vehicle. As I passed by one of the campus buildings, I noticed a man who fell in behind me. As I turned to look, he put his hand over his head. All I could see was long black hair. Of course, it was the eighties, so everyone had a mullet. He was several yards away, and the campus was always full of people, so nothing seemed too unusual. Once in the parking lot, I decided to give the follower one more look. This time, his face was not covered, and the long black hair was attached to a white, rubber, terrifying skeleton mask. The knife he held at his side was probably only a short pocket knife, but in the glow of the parking lights, it looked ten inches long. His walk had turned into a dead run straight for me. After a second or two of shock, I made a decision to scream. Opening my mouth as wide as I could, only silence emerged. I was frozen in fear. Nothing came up but a terrified gasp. My legs, however, regained composure, and I began to run toward the street. As I got closer to the sidewalk, I could feel him closing in on me. I turned and threw my keys and my Bible case at him in defense. It only slowed him down for a second, and he began charging again. I leaped over a hedge by the sidewalk when I felt a hand on my shoulder pushing me to the ground. Landing on my back, I shielded my face and upper chest from what I knew was now a fourteen-inch knife. The seconds that passed seemed like hours. He was bent over me so close that I could smell the plastic of the mask. I beat at him with my arms, screaming the only thing I knew to scream: "In Jesus's name, in Jesus's name." And just like that, he grabbed my purse and ran. He only took a few dollars and my student ID, or did he? No. He took my courage and my fighting spirit. A two-minute episode turned a strong, independent young woman into a paranoid, jittery coward. Coming out of this relatively unscathed was a miracle. What didn't come out, though, was—you guessed it—the halo.

The incident left me obviously shaken and very untrusting of people. But, as everyone says, time heals all wounds, and I bounced back—yet again. It's amazing how women have a need to regain control in their life, and no matter how many times we are held underwater, we keep floating back to the top. It was during one of these floating seasons that I met my soon-to-be husband. Growing up in a little town, you know everybody, and there was a man about eleven years older than me that seemed to be the catch of the county. He had a little boy from a previous marriage, had a good job, and a nice house. He had a charming personality. Everyone loved him. Well, as you might suspect, we began dating and dated for about the last two years I was in college. He asked me to marry him, and I happily agreed. We got married within a few weeks of graduation, and life was blissfully happy. We both had thriving careers. I worked as a district manager for a clothing company, and he was a manager for various asphalt plants. We lived out of hotels and company furnished apartments and met up on weekends at our beautiful custom-built home in our little town. Six years into the marriage, child number 1 came along: a beautiful little girl with absolutely no hair. Not able to force myself to be away from her for days at a time, I quit my job and decided to be a stay-at-home mom. The next year, a strapping baby boy appeared, and life was fantastic with our picture-perfect family. My husband's son came to live with us, and I was the mightiest supermom you've ever seen. Toting two toddlers and chauffeuring a teenager was busy work to say the least. My husband worked a couple hours away and had an apartment in the city, but we saw each other as much as we could. I didn't mind being the stay-at-home mommy, and I certainly stayed busy, but after a few months of being home with three children, I grew antsy. This life was not for me. I went back to college and earned a teaching certification. Within a couple years I was a schoolteacher, just like my mom, and I couldn't have been more proud. Even though our lives were thrust into fast forward with the busyness of children and careers, we still attended church together. I became closer and closer to God and volunteered with vacation Bible school and even started a youth ministry. After a few years, some drastic changes took place. I felt God call me into the ministry. We opened a church, I became a licensed minister, my husband got promoted, and we sold our home and began building our dream home. With so many hopes and plans on the horizon, I was the most blessed woman in the world. Life had taken a turn for the better. After thirteen years of wedded bliss, my halo was definitely back and shinning brighter than ever. I felt safe and protected. I would boast of my happy marriage and my faithful husband. He called every night at eight sharp to tell all of us how much he loved us. I even spoke at various churches and women's groups on how to make marriage last and familys that stay together. Well, as you might expect, there was a thief lurking in the shadows that I did not see. During the time our first house sold and before the second one was ready, something unexpected happened. Hints that my husband was not faithful began to creep into my mind. I can't tell you exactly why and what spurred them on. All I know is that I had a feeling he was cheating, and it wasn't the first time. After a little sleuthing and spying, I discovered thirty or more pornographic DVDs in his apartment, along with women's accessories, alcohol, and hidden money. I waited it out for a few weeks with more investigating. I discovered gambling was a habit, and he frequented the casinos and bars often. After confronting him and going back and forth with accusing each other, he finally confessed. My husband sat me down and read me a four-page letter admitting his separate life. He confessed to having over ten different affairs. He had a whole separate life in the city I knew nothing about. He had been with women he knew, women he didn't, women from the city, and women from our little country town. Breaking my heart even further, he admitted to an affair with his brother's girlfriend, who eventually married his brother and became a sister-in-law. I guess I must have overlooked the knowing glances they shared at family barbeques. How long had I played the fool? After we separated, women began coming out of the woodwork that had been with my husband. Seeing them at the grocery store was, as you can imagine, a little more than uncomfortable. The hardest truth came when he confessed to instigating an affair with my brother's wife. She never gave in to him, but my brother and sister-in-law kept their distance once they knew what kind of man he was. They felt they couldn't tell me for whatever reason. For years my husband led me to believe my brother had just changed and was perhaps getting big-headed from his new job. "He's got his big shot job, and he doesn't have time for us anymore," he would say of my big bro. I believed these lies about my brother for years until I learned the truth. What kind of man drives a wedge in your family just to cover his sin? Of course, my husband admitted to everything and expressed great remorse for his behavior. He claimed his undying love for me and that he would change. He tossed all the pornography in the dumpster and even volunteered to quit his job. But how can one trust again after that? It was as if I had been married for thirteen years to a man I didn't know. I felt as if I had been unknowingly married to a mob king and had found dead bodies in my basement. Who was this man? Who was this stranger? I wandered around for days, just lost. I couldn't eat or sleep and dropped twenty-five pounds in a week. I felt I had to stop preaching and took a leave from the church we had built with such care. We separated, and I debated over whether to divorce or give him another chance. After two weeks, he began seeing someone else, so I opted for divorce. I received criticism and condemnation from people in my community. But no one has to live your life. No one knows your anguish. God knows, and he is the one you turn to for answers in this time. The pain was too great. The knife in the back had been thrust in too far. Sometimes, there is no turning back, even if you want to. There are times in life when you have to let go of the very thing that is drowning you, even when it is all you have to hold on to. This was the place I was at when my son barged in with the broken ranger. My halo was not only gone; I didn't think I'd ever see it again.

My story is no worse than anyone else's, and I would never claim my hurt was deeper either. I simply shared my experiences so all the readers would know I have been there and I know the pain that accompanies such betrayals. When your spouse is unfaithful, abusive, or selfish, the halo that holds your trust, your worth, and your identity is ruthlessly ripped off and tossed in a gutter. So many women I've spoken with feel the same way. When your whole identity is tied up in being a wife and a mother, and that identity is smashed, then who are you? Women struggle to find themselves again. It is because their halo is gone, and without it, they don't know how to behave, act, dream, or live. Women find themselves doing very strange things or showing very odd behaviors after such a betrayal. They are simply not themselves. However, there is good news; the halo isn't lost forever. It isn't destroyed either. It can be retrieved.

2

Thieves in Our Midst

There are all kinds of thieves in the world. After working for several years as a district manager for a large clothing chain, I got a firsthand look at the magnitude of shoplifting. I thought I was so wise I could spot a shoplifter within seconds of their entry. While I did become quite adept at reading the signs of retail theft, I was ignorant about the ways of a heart thief. Someone rarely notices a burglar in their emotional life until after the robbery has occurred and their valuables are gone forever. This chapter will attempt to identify all the halo thiefs who may have broken into your life and stolen your innocence and dreams and all those who may appear in the future.

Closest to Home

I believe that every person should have a license to become a parent. I wish there were some kind of a test to give to prospecting parents to decide if they have what it takes to endure parenthood. Unfortunately, parents can be some of the biggest thieves. They can abandon the child and make them feel like they weren't worth the effort. Verbal, physical, and sexual abuse are the worst thefts by parents. The emotional scars left behind can damage a child for life if they don't learn how to heal. Children of abuse are often left feeling very insecure, terribly unloved, and withdrawn. However, many can become the opposite and be extremely angry, bitter, untrusting, hostile, and unforgiving. These types of abuse leave a child feeling not just as a piece of litter tossed out the window, but rather as a piece of trash ripped to shreds and then lit on fire. No one can truly know how damaging and deep the scars of such ruthless treatment are. I'm convinced that even the victim is unaware of some of the inner trauma and disfigurement that occurred in the psyche of their mind and soul. Regardless of the resulting behavior and character that develops, they are not the person they were born to be. God created all of us to be perfect, special, worthy, holy, kind, loving, forgiving, trusting, and humble. Yet he also created us to be victorious, powerful, bold, prosperous, and conquerors. And we were all exactly that person at some point in time. But through careless or merciless hands, God's creation became transfigured. In short, the halo was stolen, and those children are far from who they were destined to be.

Stalking Strangers

As in the incident of the man with the knife on my college campus, strangers have the ability to catch you unaware and steal your halo so fast you don't know what happened. As a high school teacher, I have the opportunity to teach many young women. I have had numerous young ladies share horrific stories of rape and other attacks. One wouldn't think it would happen at such an alarming rate, especially in the rural area in which I teach; however, sexual assault is happening everywhere. Every 107 seconds someone is sexually assaulted. 68% of all sexual attacks are not reported and those that are go unpunished. 98% of rapists never spend a day in jail. One out of every six American woman have been the victim of an attempted rape or completed rape in her lifetime. Nine out of ten victims are female.

Sex trafficking is one of the largest growing criminal enterprises in the world today. 20.9 million adults and children are bought and sold worldwide. Women and girls make up 98% of trafficking victims. In a world in which we have come so far with women's rights and protecting freedoms, we have failed miserably at protecting women. Young women and girls disappear at an alarming rate all across the globe. To many men, they are seen as nothing more than an object to be used, abused, and thrown away at their discretion. Pornography feeds this industry. Many of the girls abducted are forced to make pornographic videos or pose for pictures. The escalating use of pornography fuels the demand for girls. Where there is a demand, there will always be someone willing to provide the supply. Most people think pornography is innocent. They believe it is a harmless way to release sexual urges. However, not all girls on the TV, video, or Internet are highly paid actresses free to come and go as they please. Most are forced into these acts to feed a three-hundred-billion–dollar-a-year industry. Pornography has a price, and young women and girls from the age of six and up have to pay that price with their bodies and lives every single day.

We should be outraged that crimes against women are not only occurring but escalating at an alarming rate. Whether it is a one-time incident or a lifetime of sexual captivity, these women and young girls have had their freedom stripped, their voice silenced, and their halos ripped off mercilessly.

The statistics show that these women often have mental health issues after the incident. They are

- Three times for likely to suffer from depression
- Six times more likely to suffer from post-traumatic stress disorder
- Thirteen times more likely to abuse alcohol
- Twenty-six times more likely to abuse drugs
- Four times more likely to commit suicide

When will we rise up as a nation and as a world and say enough is enough? The silent and often ashamed cries of these women must be broadcasted from every government in the world. Protection for those who can't protect themselves must become a priority in our political, judicial, and law enforcement systems. Stalking strangers must be stopped and receive the maximum amount of punishment.

The One Who Stole Your Heart

The most common thief in a woman's life is a man whom she trusts. It is the one to who she's given her heart. Of course, the opposite can happen as well, and women can do just as much damage in a relationship. However, victimized women seem to have a more difficult time overcoming such betrayal. Why is it that as we get older, we sometimes become more vulnerable? As children, even though we don't have coping skills, we sometimes can forget, forgive, and carry on, but as adults, the hurt lingers for what seems like forever. Boyfriends, fiancés, and husbands comprise the largest pool of robbers. Sometimes, they take your halo on purpose, and sometimes, it is accidental, but either way, your halo is gone, and it's very difficult to retrieve.

Selfishness, abuse, adultery, and pornography are among the top crimes in relationship demise. I know of several women whose lives have been destroyed by a selfish mate. Women are typically the givers and the peacemakers. We enjoy seeing others needs met and will put our own needs and wants on a back-burner to ensure everyone else gets theirs met first. Some of the ways we give without expecting in return are giving up our favorite TV show or paying all the bills so someone else's life would be more enjoyable or easier. These generous acts are wonderful and can bless people tremendously, but when they are expected, demanded, or taken for granted over a period of time, they become stolen property and services. For example, a dear friend of mine, who I'll call Katie, was in this situation. She took care of the kids, the house, and the chores. She worked and also went to school. She cooked supper every night, did all the laundry, and tried to have a smile on her face when her husband came home. While her spouse was not abusive, unfaithful, or even sarcastic, he was very selfish. He refused to take the kids to their functions and never cooked supper or performed household chores. He would spend any extra income on new hunting and fishing gadgets for himself, and the TV was tuned into his channels at all times. Katie was trying desperately just to keep her head above water while working her way to finishing a college degree. The last straw came when he insisted she quit school and get a full-time job so they could have more spending money. While Katie's life may not sound horrible, her halo was being stolen piece by piece over the years. Her husband was stripping her of her education, her dreams, her hopes, and her joy. He was smothering her with a pillow of selfishness. Many times throughout their marriage, Katie would complain about feeling neglected, unloved, being taken for granted, and being exhausted. As in most troubling marriages, things improved for a short time. He would help out a little more, attend a few of the children's sporting events, and take a short sabbatical from his hunting and fishing expeditions. But eventually, his selfishness returned, and the burden of oppression returned for Katie.

This kind of selfish attitude occurs in millions of relationships. One person becomes the doormat for the other. Many women don't know how to fix it or stop it, so they just succumb to it. They are left feeling depressed, miserable, bitter, unloved, and frustrated. While this type of halo theft is not as disastrous as some of the others, it does leave a person feeling used and unworthy, a feeling no person should ever have to deal with.

Abuse is another one of life's smashing rocks that has the potential to cause extreme breaks, not only in the bones, but in the spirit and heart as well. Physical and emotional abuse in marriage has been a problem for centuries. Years ago, women in these horrible situations didn't feel they had a way out. Divorce was not accepted, so they just put up with it and ultimately became nothing more than a whipping post for a person without a sense of decency. Fortunately, today, the topic of spouse abuse is of greater concern, and punishments are somewhat imposed upon the perpetrator. While there are some repercussions for the abuser, the abused often goes unnoticed. When a victimized woman gets out of an abusive relationship we comment, "Thank God she's out of there." But is she really? She may be out of the abusive situation physically, but many times the abuse continues to haunt the heart, mind, and soul for years to come. Escaping physically is the easy part. Escaping mentally is much tougher. The bruises, cuts, and aches of the physical body heal much more quickly than those imbedded in the heart.

Women who are abused, whether physically or emotionally, are oftentimes still enslaved after they manage to escape. Some of the resulting wounds include shame, fear, worthlessness, and low self-esteem. To be used as a punching bag for no reason by someone who claims to love you is one of the worst feelings a woman can have. To feel totally helpless and trapped like a wounded caged animal is devastating. It's no wonder so many surviving victims are diagnosed with depression, become addicted to drugs and prescription medicine, or hide away from the world. Their halos have not only been stolen, they've been crushed, and the once beautiful and confident angel stares down at her halo with hopelessness. How can she ever live again? She can. Through the love of God, she most certainly can.

Adultery is yet another theft that can occur in your home. According to recent surveys, 41% of all marriages experience some kind of infidelity. Husbands have a higher percentage of adultery than the wives. Yet again, let me make myself clear that male or female can participate in this sin, but for the focus of this book, the woman will be seen as the victim. A husband who has a one-time affair or a lifetime of indiscretion is really inconsequential when it comes to the pain that is experienced. When a man and a woman vow to be faithful, and one keeps the promise and the other one doesn't, a breach of trust has occurred that cannot be fixed with a Band-Aid. I have heard from so many women who have experienced a cheating husband, and the comments about their emotions are almost always the same. They feel as though they are not enough, not pretty enough, and undesirable. Their self-esteem is at an all-time low, no matter how confident they appear to be. Inside, there is a deep sense of rejection and hurt no matter how tough their exterior seems.

Why do spouses cheat? There could be a hundred reasons and a thousand excuses, and I'm sure millions of women have heard them all. Some may seem valid, and others seem ludicrous, but in my opinion, the reason doesn't matter. The end result is what matters. The intention doesn't make the pain any less painful.

Pornography is a form of cheating. The world tries to tell us such activity is not harmful. It tries to convince us a little sexual lust, when not acted upon, can actually be healthy. It provides a man a release for stress, frustration, and tension. But that is bull! These statistics on pornography may shock you.

- 30% of the Internet industry is pornography.
- Porn sites get more visitors each month than Netflix, Amazon, and Twitter combined.
- More than 64% of men admit to regular viewing of pornography.
- Men are 54% more likely to look at porn than women.
- Online porn watching contributes to over half of all divorces.

Pornography, in any shape or form, is a cancer that will eventually destroy a marriage and the person engaging in it. Jesus said that any one who looks upon a woman with lust has already committed adultery in his heart. It doesn't matter if the husband agrees with Christ's statement or not. Adultery has been committed, and the results of such unfaithfulness are the same as if he physically engaged with another person. The mental and spiritual damage the wife goes through when her husband engages in pornography is the same as if she's been cheated on physically. She feels unworthy and undesirable. If she's aware of her husband's viewing habits, then she may feel unclean or dirty when they are together. She may feel used and/or feel as though she is a substitute for the woman in the magazine or on the screen. The result: halo theft, a broken ranger, a hurting wife, and an injured child of God.

Those who claim to be your soulmate can throw the largest of all smashing asteroids. The one who promises to love, honor, cherish, and forsake all others has now become the one who cheats, lies, degrades, and clings to someone or something else. The one who initially stole you heart and took your breath away is also the one who stole your halo.

He Comes to Steal

It is very convenient to blame the low-down, no-count scum of a guy that stole your halo. It's awfully easy to accuse a flesh-and-blood human person because they're here, and we can see and touch them. We know what they did, and there is no denying it. However, the individual who has harmed you is not solely the one to blame. While I'm not excusing anyone of his behavior, there exists another person behind the scenes causing much of the problem. There was and still is a bigger thief in your life. Your mate or spouse may have been simply following commands given by someone else. Who else could possibly want to hurt you so much that he would go to such lengths to use another as a pawn in an evil plot against you?

Will the Real Robber Please Stand Up?

The person responsible for your hurt, and the individual pulling all the strings is none other than Lucifer, the fallen angel. The Bible tells us it is Satan himself who is out to destroy us. The book of John says, "The thief comes only to steal and kill and destroy; but I came that they may have life and have it in abundance" (John 10:10, NAS). The devil has a special vendetta against the woman. Through Mary, Jesus was born. She birthed a miracle. Women have the capability of birthing miracles every day. While both parents play a part in impacting a child's life, the mother, I believe, has the most influence. She is the first bond and fierce protector of that baby. In the animal kingdom, the female nurtures and cares for the young. She is also the fighter if danger comes. She will give up her life fighting for her children. The devil knows the bond a woman has with her children, and if he can destroy the woman, he can destroy the child. If he can destroy the child, he can destroy the world. It all starts with the woman. If the devil's sole purpose is to try to destroy you, then he is responsible for stealing your halo. It is Satan who has deceived others into hurting you. The Bible also says the devil is the accuser of the brethren. He'll not only entice another to cause you harm, either indirectly or directly, but he will then turn around and accuse you, making it seem as though it was somehow your fault. He is also the master of lies. If you've ever been lied to by someone you thought you could trust, understand that the whole concept of lying came about through the devil. The real culprit is the old cunning serpent.

Please don't think I'm excusing all misbehavior of individuals who do wrong by placing the blame on the devil. While Satan is responsible for enticing, lying, deceiving, tempting, and more, people must allow themselves to be used. When an individual cheats on his spouse, he ultimately makes the decision to engage in such activity. The devil brought the temptation, encouraged the sin, and spoke to him in ways that made it seem okay. In other words, he was an accomplice in the crime. The devil wants to steal your life, your hopes, your dreams, your confidence, your faith, and your trust, but he needs a human being to perform the robbery. Not just anyone can be used of the devil, only people that either open themselves to him or are oblivious of him. The Bible says the devil roams the earth to and fro seeking whom he may devour (1 Pet. 5:8). Closer examination reveals a master mind that is looking for an individual with certain qualities. He cannot destroy or use anyone. The word *may* indicates the devil needs a sort of foothold or permission if you will. Satan may not use just anyone; he may only use those who allow it. Most people don't think they are being used as a chess piece in the devil's game. For example, a man may cheat on his spouse but justify his actions by accusing the wife of being too busy with the children to give him any attention. A man may engage in pornography and justify his actions by claiming what he is doing isn't necessarily wrong because no one is getting physically hurt and, besides, other people do a lot worse. An abuser may defend his actions by blaming the wife for angering him. A selfish, self-absorbed spouse may feel justified to spend every other night out with the buddies by telling himself he works hard and needs a break. The devil is not going to come right out and tell these men they are being baited. He isn't going to correct the misassumption by popping up one day and exclaiming, "Oh, no, I'm partially to blame for what you're doing." The devil is not going to be the fall guy. In fact he is perfectly happy playing behind the scenes. If he can twist the truth by making someone believe their actions are justified, all the while remaining anonymous, then he can continue to manipulate for many more years. Satan actually loves it when people think he doesn't even exist. Do you see what kind of a mastermind you are up against? He deceives others into stealing your halo while very subtly convincing them they are justified, all the while blaming everyone else and, to top it off, acting invisible. How's that for an enemy!

The devil will use anyone who will give him an opening to become your mortal enemy. Don't think the flesh-and-blood man who hurt you will get off scot-free, though. There is a price to pay for partnering with the devil. The Bible says you will reap what you sow (Gal. 6:7). If the person who hurt you does not repent, their own sin will bring calamity into their lives. In fact, the devil is probably using someone else to tear them down at this very moment.

But What If I'm the Thief?

Up to this point, we've talked about all sorts of robbers and the hurt they cause. But what happens when you are the thief? That's right. We can be our own worst enemy sometimes. Have you ever run your own life in the ditch by the decisions you made? I know a woman who has done precisely this. Her name is Kerri, and she was a beautiful young woman. She had her whole life ahead of her. She came from a loving family and was financially stable and smart. Unfortunately, her dad passed away from an illness. To cope with her loss, she turned to drugs. She became an addict very quickly, and little by little she threw her halo away and to this day has not been able to find it. She used harder and harder drugs as the years went by. When she was younger, she talked of going to college and all the dreams she had. By the time she realized how much of her life she wasted, she didn't know how to get it back. She tried to quit the drugs, but it was so difficult she turned to prescription medications. Now, her health is practically destroyed, and she is miserable. She can never work or have children. Her halo is hidden well.

I believe there are Kerris all over the world. Perhaps the story is different, but many, many women throw their halos away. Most are oblivious to the potential damage it can cause. They let down their guard and engage in some type of sin they might not even consider harmful. The devil talks to them subtly and tells them the activity they are tempted with will be fun and harmless. It is all a conniving lie to strip women of their identity and self-worth.

I've seen many young women just like Kerri who think they are on top of their game, yet are losing horribly. They think they know it all, yet they're ignorant. They think their life is under control, yet it is careening off a steep cliff. In other words, they don't know their halo has been stolen. Being a high school teacher, I can see the beginning of stolen halos at a very young age. When I ask students if they are happy being exactly who they are right now, many will raise their hands. While a side of me is pleased they are so confident in themselves, another side wonders who they are confident in. Some of these young ladies are promiscuous party girls. Some are on drugs, some have a nasty disposition, and others have an "I don't care" attitude. They think their character traits are a manifestation of who they were born to be. When we discuss issues of child abuse, dysfunctional families, or date rape, many of the girls with issues raise their hands to share their experiences in these areas. They know they've been hurt or affected in some way, but they don't know they've been changed. Still others claim they come from a perfect family but are engaging in dangerous activities. They too may act negative and rebellious, claiming "That's just the way I am." These personality traits are not hereditarily embedded in the DNA of a little girl. While we all have different talents, looks, and varying personalities, we were not born with flaws. God created us all unique but perfect. He made us all different but splendid. Understand you are the way you are not because of genetics, but perhaps because of an intruder that stole your identity. Jesus Christ will help you gain back your lost soul.

The devil doesn't want you to see his part in your dilemma. He wants you to think you made every decision by yourself. He'll tell you that you are doing fine just the way you are, and if people don't like who you are, then to hell with them. If you do realize you don't like who you've become and how your life is turning out, he'll tell you that you made your bed and now lie in it. The devil is so sneaky he convinces you to throw your halo away, and then he buries it so deep you don't know where to begin looking.

One lady I talked with said, "I've thrown everything away, no one cares about me anymore, why should I even live." If you are perhaps feeling the same, don't stop living, don't give up, and don't quit. There is good news: you can gain back what has been stolen.

So what do you do if you're like I was during my college years and you threw your halo away? Realize that you, just like any other thief, had an accomplice: the devil. It's not all your fault, no matter what everyone else may tell you. The horrible things you may have done weren't you. You were acting as a different person. You were under the influence of the drug of lies and deception. You were manipulated, controlled, and being used. While that fact does not let you off the hook and you may still have to suffer through some of the consequences of your actions, it can hopefully help you to see yourself in a different light. You were never a monster, only a victim. For example, when a child is abused, don't blame the child. Don't blame yourself either. You have an abuser that is out to kill, steal, and destroy you, your family, your finances, your hope, your joy, and, ultimately, your life. Realize how you've been deceived and do something about it. Tell the devil you are not his pawn anymore. Step out of his control. You may feel like you are taking a step into the great unknown. You may feel like there is no hand held out to you in help. Everyone may have turned their back on you, but there is one hand that has always been there. There is a hand that has been stretched out to you since day 1. It is a hand of love, compassion, mercy, grace, forgiveness, and power. It is the only hand that can take you out of the pit and place you on a mountain of hope. It is a hand that will go with you to search the darkest places for your halo. It is a hand that will never forsake you or let you go. It is a hand with a nail scar in the center of the palm and your name engraved in it. Grab hold of the hand of Jesus Christ today and begin the journey to becoming a new creature.

3

I Can Do It by Myself

I remember my daughter during her toddler years. She was so stubborn and independent. Every time I tried to help her tie her shoes or fasten her seat belt, she would push me away and say, "I can do it by myself." Sometimes, it was a painstakingly long process as she fumbled to do it alone. Unfortunately, as adults, we haven't changed much. Sadly, many women decide not to take the hand of Jesus. They think they can fix themselves with only their strong will and determination. Women believe they can get their halo back all by themselves. What results is a halfway patch-up job. Millions of women have tried other cures and fixes, but they don't work for long. Just as my son's broken ranger was fixed with super glue and duct tape, it will never be just like new. The little action figure is still vulnerable to break again with the slightest bit of strain. You too will continue to fall apart unless you have a permanent repair.

Going after Other Gods

Opening yourself to a new religion may be a repair some women try. Going after other gods never leads to restoration. It only leads down another dark alley where you search for your halo, only to find someone or something else lurking there to tear you apart. Buddhism, Wicca, and New Age theology all may have positive points and good attributes, but they don't have a savior. They don't have someone who holds all the answers. The Bible says that Jesus Christ is the way, the truth, and the life (John 14:6). He is the only one who can take you from ground zero to a shinning tall skyscraper again. He is the only one, and the gospel message is the only thing that is real. That is where you halo is. If you want it back, that is the only place to go.

Advice Givers

Some patch-up jobs many women try include taking advice from others. If this advice is coming from a Spirit-filled believer, then by all means take it. If the advice follows the word of God, then it is sound, but you must check the source before attempting any medical repair on your heart and soul. The first form of patch job comes from a friend. After an injuring blow, sometimes the only source of comfort a girl can find is with her girlfriends. Thank God for best friends who are always there to pick up the pieces. But from what I've witnessed through the years, many females are receiving advice and repair jobs from another broken ranger. No one intentionally tries to put you back together haphazardly, but if they don't know how to repair themselves, how can they ever repair you?

The super glue of life can come in many forms. I know I've received all sorts of advice that wasn't appropriate, but I took it anyway because it sounded good. Besides, my friend had gone through the same situation I had. She ought to know what to do, right? In reality, it was the blind leading the blind. One bit of superglue I tried was "Get back in the saddle again." Another was "Get back at him." Still another sounded like this: "Get over it." Many of you may have heard the same advice. While it all sounds good and may work temporarily, the injury still exists. Other friends I know have tried the glue of illegal or prescription drugs. These patch jobs just cover up the cut like a Band-Aid. They may stay on for a while, but sooner or later they fall off, and the scar is still there. When that happens, the pain and hurt can come rushing back, and you may feel just as vulnerable and depressed as when the incident first occurred.

Back in the Saddle Again

A new intimate relationship is another patch-up job many women try. Jumping into relationship after relationship isn't going to help. You may find yourself in a worse mess than before. Through my lifetime, I would jump into the arms of any man who showed the slightest bit of protective care over me. The care wasn't real; it was only a ruse to win the game. I was no more than a prize at the end of the challenge. Once the conquest was over, there was no need to continue the charade of love. I have been duped by more men than I can count. If you've ever watched *Pretty Woman* with Julia Roberts, then you know what I'm talking about. She made a comment in the movie that revealed her own naivety: "If there was a bum within a fifty-mile radius, I was attracted to him." That was me. I was the bum magnet. Going from guy to guy is never the way to fix a broken heart. Those other guys don't have your halo. And, many times, they don't care that you lost it. They won't try to help you get it back either. However, you don't have to be a spinster all your life. God doesn't want you to never trust and never love again. Just be careful who you choose.

Revenge Time

Getting even is probably one of the worst forms of repair you can choose. All revenge does is pull you down to the level of your thief. Bitterness and unforgiveness are the platforms from which revenge operates. I have been in and out of bitterness for years. I used to get so angry at my ex that I would almost give myself an ulcer over it. I would think of the next scathing remark I might say the next time

I had the opportunity. Pinterest is filled with quotes about revenge. I had them all pinned to my board. Instead of focusing on things that would uplift my soul, I focused on the hurt and bitterness. This blocks the blessings of God.

Get Over It

The "get over it" phrase is one many hurl your way in the form of tough-love advice. It sounds good but can be impossible to achieve. This patch-up job comes without tools to accomplish the task. If you don't have the tools or skills to control your mind, feelings, and emotions, then this piece of advice is too difficult. Along this same line, others may encourage you to deal or cope with the hurt. Again, dealing and coping takes skill, and without the skills, repair is a lengthy and painful process. For example, could you fill in a hole the size of an Olympic swimming pool without equipment? A loader and dump truck could take care of this problem in a day or two. Even a shovel and wheelbarrow could make headway after a long period of time. But if you had to scoop dirt by hand, no doubt it would be a lifelong project. At the end of each day, you would be dirty and exhausted. That is what happens to people who take the "get over it" advice without skills, knowledge, or tools. Counselors, therapists, and psychiatrists oftentimes give out tools, help you acquire the knowledge, and teach you valuable skills to make the job easier, but unless the advice is Christian-based, you could be in for a break again.

Deal with It

This "deal with it" advice can also come from your robber. I'm sure you can identify with the following situation. A friend of mine named Tammy had been cheated on by her spouse. She couldn't take the rejection and decided to divorce him. She still loved him but couldn't handle the embarrassment, shame, pain, and abuse of trust. Having children together, they still needed to communicate about various things. Tammy had a difficult time talking to him about anything. Fighting was common, and she would inevitably bring up his affairs, to which he responded with one of the following: "Just let it go," "Why do you keep bringing it up?" "I said I was sorry," "Well, I wanted to stay and work it out, but you wanted the divorce," or "Drop it, it's in the past now." It was in the past for him, but for Tammy, the pain was still very much in the present. Just because she got her freedom back through a divorce didn't mean she got her halo back. A person cannot destroy your self-esteem, crash your life, and then expect you to just act like the whole thing never happened.

While this reaction from a thief is common with divorced couples, it is more common with couples who stay together. If a woman stays with her thief, the road ahead is not always smooth. But for some strange reason, men seem to think it should be. They feel that by confessing, admitting, and seeking help, the problem is then taken care of, and everything should return to normal and be hunky-dory. I've heard men make comments such as, "Well if you've forgiven me, then why do you keep bringing it up?" "If we're going to try to work this out, then why don't you trust me?" or "If we're going to stay together, why are you still so sad?" For some reason men, expect to be pardoned for all their crimes quickly. Women are made to feel like they should just get over it, deal with it, or cope, but do it in a hurry. I've even heard other women criticize fellow women for not being able to snap out of it. The assumption today is that if you say you're going to stay with your spouse after they've harmed you in some way, then you should just put all hurts, all fears, all anger, and all trust issues behind you and forget anything ever happened. Ladies, for those of you who are receiving this advice or hearing these comments, listen up. You are not a puppet. Your emotions and feelings cannot be controlled by someone else's desires. Only you can decide when you can trust again. Only you know when you feel comfortable again. You can't just put on a happy face because you think it's expected. You are the one who decides when you're healed. Now don't take this as an excuse to make your spouse's life miserable forever. The truth is, if you decide to work this out, then at some point in time you do have to get over it. But don't let anyone tell you it should happen quickly and painlessly. It might occur in precisely that way, and you could be the type of person that forgets and trusts immediately. If so, praise God for your generous and trusting nature.

Most women however, cannot get their halo back that quick. I'm always amazed when I hear men talking about how their wife should deal with what has occurred when they are to blame. Complaining about your spouse not being able to whip her emotions back into place is similar to misuse of an automobile. You can't take a car and run it hard, never change the oil, never rotate the tires, slam the doors, beat on the hood, run it off a cliff, and then expect it to look new and run in perfect condition. It won't happen. Without extensive repairs and body work by the hands of a trained mechanic, that car may never be like it was. Yet men think they can steal your halo, dent it, smash it, and throw it in a brush pile somewhere and expect you to go find it, put it back together, spit shine it up, and plop it on your head without tilting. During my marriage, I remember thinking, *You broke me, now you want me to mend by myself and do it in a jiffy.* That kind of an expectation is not only unreasonable; it is selfishly demanding.

Unfortunately it is not just robbers and friends who give this advice. The church is guilty as well. I'm not criticizing the church of which love, compassion, and mercy are an integral part of their community. I'm condemning the self-righteous church. I'm knocking the church that is more loyal to rules and laws than it is to the Lord and Savior. Sometimes, an injured person flies to the comfort of a church body, seeking help for their wounded spirit, and the advice given is cruel and uncaring. They may be told to stay with their spouse because God hates divorce. While it is true that God does hate divorce, he also hates abuse, adultery, pornography, selfishness, and pride. The pastor of that church does have a responsibility to feed the sheep. He or she should be advising based on Scripture, but love and compassion should lead the way. Sometimes, women don't have a choice. If their spouse wants a divorce, there is nothing they can do to stop it. Should they be condemned because of something beyond their control? Still others must make the decision for themselves. The church can encourage a decision, but everyone must make their own choices in life. Ultimately, everyone has to answer to God for their own decisions. Bear in mind, God did give allowable reasons for divorce. So if God gives the permission, who is the church to disagree?

Forced Personalities

When others try to force their opinions on you and give you unsound, unbiblical advice, what results is a different personality. Women who have had their halo stolen have lost their identity. Their self-esteem is destroyed, and they don't know who they are anymore. So, in order to cope or deal, they adopt a different character. I refer to it as a forced personality. Instead of a split personality or multiple personality, in which there are two or more characters living inside one mind, a forced personality is only one type of mind-set that you pigeonhole yourself into. For example, in order to cope or deal with your pain, you adopt a tough-girl persona. This personality claims to be harsh, uncaring, and untrusting. It is only a façade, or an outer shell, to protect you from further injury. Others may adopt a personality of weakness. They allow their injury to continue to haunt them for years. They talk about it all the time, and they blame everything on their horrible past. They become a victim. They expect others to hurt them because that's just the way life has treated them. As a result, they usually become a victim time and time again. Their halo becomes stolen over and over and over. Most of the time, they cause the hurt. Victimized women who choose to live as a victim invite bitterness, distrust, and depression. Let me give you an example of this type of personality. Clara was an acquaintance of mine. Her husband left her for another woman. She totally lost it. She became addicted to prescription drugs, illegal drugs, alcohol, and all other destructive behavior. When she finally came to her senses, she didn't use anymore, but she blamed all her problems on her ex-spouse. She jumped into a new relationship but continued to compare him with her ex. She didn't trust, continued to be depressed, accused him of adultery, and basically made his life miserable. When he finally left, she made the statement, "Well, I knew he would leave, he's just like my ex. All men are. They can't be trusted." Carrying your baggage into your next relationship sets you up for failure every time. Don't become a broken ranger repeatedly.

Still another forced personality comes in the form of homosexuality or bisexual behavior. A woman who has been hurt by a man, or by several men, may feel this alternative lifestyle is a safer option. But it isn't. It isn't an alternative lifestyle either. It is sin and is an abomination to God. It is a forced personality that you adopted because you were lost and afraid. You were not created to be homosexual; no one is. You were created in God's image with a special halo of marvelous traits and abilities.

There are many more forced personalities that women adopt in order to cope with issues in their life. If you've adopted a personality that isn't the one God intended for you to display, it's not too late. You can change. You can become a new, better, and improved person. All the bad advice you've tried and all the different characters you've adopted doesn't change the person God really created you to be. The real you is still out there. Your halo is yet to be retrieved. Take a step back from all the garbage that has infected your life. Take a break from all the bad advice. Rip off all the old Band-Aids. They are only covering the hurt. You don't need a faulty patch job or another form of medicine. What you need is a miracle. There's good news: God has a personal miracle in store for you. Open yourself up to receive it.

4

Search and Seizure

Have you ever lost something of value and launched an all-out search and seizure mission to find it? I am probably the worst at misplacing and forgetting things. I've locked my keys in my car countless times. I've misplaced jewelry, my phone, paperwork, and more. Someone will tell me something, and I'll forget it two minutes later. I'll go into a room to do or get something and then forget why I'm there. Thank goodness I've never misplaced my children. I've been called ditzy, scatterbrained, and, of course, a dumb blonde. I think lots of women, especially moms, have been labeled similar at some point in time. Personally, I think women multitask so well that sometimes we take it to an extreme. We have so many things going on inside our mind when we hit maximum load capacity that some things are bound to get lost. Losing things of importance, however, can become a critical and even a life-changing issue. I lost my keys at a Mexican restaurant one time. I accidentally left them on my tray when I threw my trash away. Walking to the van with my mother, I realized I didn't have my keys. Searching through my purse, my mother's purse, our table—the horrid thought finally dawned on me: Perhaps they were in the very large, very nasty, trash can. Having only one set of keys, and desperate to retrieve them, we shamefully had to ask the order takers if we may rummage through the trash can. Although disgusting, one bag of trash wouldn't be too difficult. But, no, the devil made sure I would endure much worse. It just so happened that one of the restaurant workers had emptied all the trash cans during our previous search. Now we were directed to the garbage dumpster. About four large trash bags sat on top. As my mother and I looked at one another, we each groaned a low sigh and grabbed the first two bags. After about an hour of digging through someone else's dripping taco sauce, spilled drinks, and leftover slop, I was thoroughly disgusted and out of hope. My keys were nowhere to be found. Going back inside to wash my hands and arms, a line worker asked if we had any luck on our search. Simply shaking my head and muttering no, I continued walking. At that time, another line worker quipped, "Hey, I found a set of keys. They were lying on a tray on top of the trash can, and I laid them behind the counter." He very casually reached over to a back counter and dangled my keys in front of me and said, "Is this them?" While part of me wanted to slap this young man, another part of me was so relieved to have my keys back I simply sighed and said, "Thank you so much." Sheepishly, I looked at my mom. She shook her head in defeated exasperation and turned away.

Sometimes we go to painstaking lengths to find a precious lost item when, in fact, it is so close. We search and search and never look in the obvious places. While searching for your halo, you may do the same thing. Seeking every possible location, searching in someone else's eyes, digging into someone else's beliefs, and hunting in places you should never go, only to come up empty. But no matter how long you've looked, don't give up. Your halo is out there. There is hope. It is being held safely in the hands of Jesus Christ. If your halo was ripped off your head in one swoop, Jesus caught it and has been keeping it safe all this time. If it was torn off piece by piece, Jesus collected the pieces as they were thrown aside. There is only one place to look for your halo. The person you were created to be—the kind, feminine, yet courageous and confident woman you were born as—is waiting to be discovered. All you have to do is look to the finder of lost halos.

The Abused Calls the Abused

Sometimes when a woman has been hurt by a man, whether it be once, twice, or a multitude of times, the last thing she wants to do is trust another man again. Yet Jesus Christ is the only man a woman can safely trust. He knows what it is like to be hurt, wounded, and used. Our Savior spent several years of his life being cursed, ridiculed, and scorned. Mobs of people tried to hurl him off a cliff. One of his dearest friends betrayed him for money. Another denied his relationship with him. He suffered the most severe case of abuse anyone has ever endured. The stripes on his back were caused by whips with spikes, nails, and pieces of rock on the ends. They tore into his flesh, gripped his skin, and then ripped it in strips from his back. The thorns, which composed the crown, were needle-shaped splinters. They used sticks and boards to force these painful spikes into his head and brow. He was undoubtedly kicked, shoved, hit, slapped, and spit upon. I'm sure there were rocks and dust thrown at him as he exhaustingly carried the cross up a hill, where even more torture awaited. His abuse did not last for a few seconds or minutes. The thick nails, which hammered into his hands and feet, held him aloft for hours. Every nerve of his body had to be raw. The pain had to be excruciating. He was strung up to die like a criminal while many looked on with disgust. He was humiliated, stripped of dignity, and dripping with sweat and blood. His body had to be racking with pain. I'm convinced that Jesus endured more torture than is really told in the Bible. Only he could give an accurate account of the abuse that occurred in the hidden chambers and dungeons while he awaited his execution. Trust me, he knows what abuse, neglect, pain, and mistreatment feel like. And perhaps, like you and me, he loved his abusers. He dearly loved the very people who, with sneering grins, stared up at him while he bled for their souls.

When you think no one understands what you've been through, there is a Savior who knows every hurt you've ever felt. When you think no one cares, there is a man reaching out to be your best and most loyal friend. Jesus has kept every secret you've ever had. He's heard every prayer you've ever prayed. He's seen every tear fall. He's felt every heartbreak. He's been there, and he knows your pain. His hand has always been reaching out to touch you. His arms have always been ready to catch every fall. Unfortunately, many women have reached in the wrong direction or fallen into another's arms. Yet he still stands ready. Jesus has known, abuse and he wants other abused children. He is searching the world over for abused and neglected people. He is calling them into his rest. Fall into his arms today, and you'll never fall again.

Jesus will never let you down. He will defend you forever. But you must trust one last time. I know how hard it is to give your heart away again, but this man will never ever hurt you. He is more than a man. He is your best friend. He is a loyal spouse. He is a Savior of your sins. He is the best surgeon in the world. He is your fiercely protective father. He is your financial provider. He is your source of joy. He is your powerful, defending lawyer. He is everything you need. He is Lord, if you will allow him to be.

Trash to Treasure

Jesus is much like a dumpster diver. He can dive into the nastiest, dirtiest, smelliest dumpsters and come out with a piece of trash that looks as though it should stay there. That piece of garbage he retrieved goes to his repair shop, and he transforms it into a thing of beauty. If you enjoy remodeling, refurbishing, or restoring projects, then you know what I mean. Recently a home burned in my neighborhood. The family took out the salvageable items and left the damaged ones sitting on the lot to haul off later. Driving by, I noticed a chair in the pile of discards. Stopping, wanting to get a closer look, I noticed that the chair was smoke stained, scratched, water damaged, torn, broken, and had missing parts. But looking beyond the external damage, I found the main structure to be strong. I rushed home and called the former owners and inquired about the pile of rubble. They were shocked I would want anything lying in that heap and invited me to haul off as much as I wanted. I was so excited I went back that same evening. As snow and sleet were falling, I rescued the old, broken chair from the pile of rejects, carefully loaded it up, and brought it home. After months of stripping burnt layers, sanding out scratches, repairing broken parts, replacing foam, pulling rusted staples and nails, and reupholstering, a chair worth thousands stood tall and proud. Once an object bound for the burn pile, it now stands elegant and proud in my foyer for all to admire. If you feel like a used-up, burnt-up torn shell of a person teetering on a pile of disaster, don't lose hope. There is a Savior named Jesus Christ who diligently searches the discards of others with the sole purpose of a beautiful restoration.

Many people don't know who Jesus really is. He is not the person sitting in a pew listening soberly to the white-robed choir sing his praises. He is not perched upon his throne casting judgmental glances at the sinful. He is not a trophy that only the elite self-righteous few display on their mantles. My Jesus is a trash-to-treasure kind of guy. He can take leftovers and make a soufflé. He can take pieces of litter and create a masterpiece. The real Lord is walking the streets calling to the prostitutes and gang members. The redeemer I know is hovering close to the gutters looking for broken, crumpled people he can swoop down and protect. My heavenly brother is knocking on crack houses, telling them he can be the most high they've ever felt. The real Jesus is looking frantically for hurting women to make new again. He is scouring the earth with halos in hand looking for you.

The Bible says in the book of Luke that he came to heal the brokenhearted. Do you have a broken heart today? Then you're in for a treat. Because the great Messiah, prophesied for centuries, was sent just for you. The Bible also reminds us that Jesus suffered the hurt, the lame, the blind, the deaf, and the poor to come to him (Luke 14:12). He wants those with issues, pains, and regrets. He wants broken rangers. He wants those without halos.

The Permanent Fix

There is only one cure-all; a permanent fix that makes you almost unbreakable. It's the love of Jesus Christ. He has held your halo the minute it was tossed aside. It may be in pieces, but he can put it all back together again. He can polish away all the spots and rust. He can cover it again with pure gold and place in on your head as a crown fit for a queen.

You may be wondering that if Jesus is the only permanent fix, why he hasn't fixed you yet? There are two steps you must take for God to help. The truth lies in step number 1: the search. While Jesus is searching for you, you must also search for him. I know there have been times my mother has been trying to get hold of me, and perhaps I'm trying to get hold of her too, but we're looking in the wrong places and calling the wrong numbers. We've missed each other's calls and messages, and our schedules didn't line up for a day or so. The same can be true when you search for your halo. To truly find Jesus Christ and your original personality, you must look in one place: the holy Bible. Going to church is wonderful, and listening to preachers and well-meaning Christians is a plus. But nothing will replace the one-on-one relationship with the Father. When you find out who

God is through his Holy Word, you are in the search mode to retrieve your halo. The second step is seizure. You need to grab hold of your new life—seize your dreams and hopes. The only way to do that is through what is called salvation. Getting saved is the only step that will lead you in the direction of restoration. It is the only permanent fix. Unfortunately, many churches don't know the meaning of salvation, and as a result, they try to offer something they aren't sure of. A church that talks salvation but doesn't fully comprehend the meaning is similar to a car salesman who knows little about the car he's selling. When I talk with Christians about salvation, I always ask a series of questions. First, "What are you saved from?" And next, "What are you saved to?" The usual answer is one of two things. Many people say saved means they have a spot reserved in heaven. The other usual response is this, "I'm saved from sin." Both of these are awesome aspects of salvation but are not the accurate meaning. The Hebrew definition of salvation is "the whole process by which man is delivered from any evil, whether physical or spiritual, that interferes with the highest blessing of God" (*Strong's Concordance*). According to that definition, heaven is included and a sin-free life is included, but so is living free from fear, worry, sickness, lack, heartache, and much more.

Many people get saved and accept only part of salvation. They may live as a new creature with new thoughts and ideas, but they may never fully realize all their hopes, goals, and dreams in this life because they do not know they are delivered from any restraint or evil holding them back. In other words, they get saved and stuck. The Bible says, "My people are destroyed for lack of knowledge" (Hosea 4:6, kjv). God calls them *his* people. He is referring to people who claim to belong to him, yet they perish because they don't know some things. Salvation is a gift that contains a life of abundance of all things. It provides a new personality, a new outlook, health, prosperity, joy, peace, and safety. Accepting true salvation is the only way to get your halo back intact.

Don't Pearl Cast

Many broken rangers will not ever fully comprehend the message of salvation and therefore keep looking for another remedy for their injured soul. The Bible warns against setting your affection or time on something other than the best. I see women who join the church yet still look to someone or something else for fulfillment. If you give your affection, time, love, money, body, or heart to someone or something else that doesn't have your best interest at heart, then you have, as the Bible says, cast your pearls before swine. You've given your halo over again to someone or something that could end up stealing it. A woman's heart should be so imbedded in Christ that a man would have to seek him to find her. Don't come to Christ as a new adventure or another experience. Becoming saved is not just another shot in the dark at happiness. It is coming home. Don't hold anything back when you come before God. He cast his only son out to be tortured for your benefit; perhaps you should cast your most precious items to him. Give him your heart in complete, unreserved measure. Don't hold anything back. Jump into the ring of fire with God, and watch how well you'll be cared for and built up. This is one guy you can cast all your pearls to. He is a collector of pearls. You may think you're stones are not very precious and you have nothing to offer him, but he's not looking at you for what you can give to him. He's looking at you for what he can give to you. He just needs you to lay down your life, your hopes, your dreams, your trust, your heart, and your family. In other words, cast all your pearls to him, and he will make the most gorgeous pearl studded halo to give back to you.

What He'll Do for You

It may seem like your situation is too far gone for God to mend. Your mind may not be able to fathom a new life and a new you. Circumstances and problems may seem so enormous that not even a miracle can budge them. When your mind cannot fathom a way, God's mind can. Consider the story of Lazarus. In the Bible there is an account of a man named Lazarus, who was a dear friend of Jesus. He had two sisters. One was named Martha, and the other was named Mary. All three loved God and accepted Jesus without reservation; however, Lazarus fell sick and died. When Jesus heard of his friend's illness, he waited a few days before coming to visit. His deliberate delay did not mean he didn't care only that he wasn't concerned with limitations. When Jesus finally arrived at Lazarus's house, he was greeted by his sister Martha with a heart-wrenching plea, "…Lord, if you had been here, my brother would not have died" (John 11: 21 NAS). Martha knew that Jesus could raise a sick man, but her faith ended when it came to raising the dead. When Jesus asked where he had been laid, they led him to the tomb. Upon his request to roll the stone away, Martha again showed her limited belief, "Lord, There will be a stench, for this time he has been dead four days, and he stinks" (John 11:39 NAS). Mary was looking at the obstacle instead of the miracle. Jesus proved to her that nothing was impossible to him as he said, "Remove the stone" (John 11:39, NAS). The onlookers were shocked as Lazarus, bandaged in burial cloths as a mummy, came wobbling out. The next statement made by Jesus is the same one he is making to you today, "…Loose him and let him go" (John 11:44, KJV). When you think your problems are a massive boulder blocking your freedom, Jesus calls to roll the stone away. When you think your past and your hurts have you bound in a shroud of despair, Jesus calls for you to be loosed and let go. When it seems like it's too late for you, remember Lazarus. Jesus can be four days late and still be on time.

One of my favorite scriptures of restoration is found in Joel 2:25. It says, "And I will restore to you the years that the locust hath eaten" (NKJV). Which means there can be things you thought were long gone, relationships you thought were destroyed, and time wasted that you can never regain, but God can restore lost items. The word of God can heal today what happened yesterday.

While Jesus is the restorer and redeemer, he is also the remover. The scriptures reveal him as the one who removed burdens and destroys yokes (Isa. 10:27). When studying Scripture, the Bible uses many analogies that would have been clearly understood by the people living in that time. During this time oxen were used often as work animals to plow the fields, pull wagons, and carry loads. A yoke was a sort of harness made of metal and leather. It was placed around the animals' neck and over the shoulders and back and was used to attach the load or wagon to. It was a restraint of sorts to keep the animal captive and useable for labor. To remove the burden from the animal would make its efforts easier. To destroy the yoke would make the animal free from burden carrying ever again. If you are carrying burdens of shame, pain, hurt, loss, addictions, or anything else, Jesus is the one who removes those. He takes all your fears, your past, your broken families, and your mistakes and unloads them. Not only does he remove your burden, but he destroys the very tool by which Satan has used to keep you enslaved. The yoke that has you tied up, restricted, or limited can be smashed to smithereens, never to be placed on you again. If you allow Christ to reign and rule in your heart, you will live a life free from bondage and without cares.

Birth a Miracle

Sometimes it's hard to believe a life of freedom and abundance can be yours. Believing that placing your hope in one man that you can't even see or touch seems ridiculous, I know. When you accept Jesus Christ with all your heart, you'll begin down a road of repair. The road may appear to be too long and too hard because everything may seem to come against you. You'll begin to doubt and second-guess your faith. To believe your life can be restored, your hopes achieved, your psyche healed, and your dreams met may look impossible, but all things are possible to those who believe (Mark 9:23). I'll not mislead you into thinking you can regain your halo back easily. While Jesus has it in his hands and has kept it for you, he'll not force you to wear it. The hard part is putting the halo back on. Stepping into the person you were created to be is much more difficult than simply knowing who you were created as. The process may be long and weary or short and painless. It all depends on you. If you've ever given birth, you know what I mean.

Some women can have a delivery that is short and relatively painless while others labor for days and push for hours. But one thing is true: to deliver a baby, you must push. The same is true for producing anything wonderful in your life. You must push through the pain, the hurt, the anxiety, and the stress. You must push through the doubts, the fears, the anger, the resentment, and the bitterness. You must push through the lonely times and through the long nights. You must push through the urges, the cravings, and the withdrawals. Jesus will always be at your side, holding your hand, wiping your brow, and encouraging you to hold on. When the devil tries to push you down into despair again, push back. Keep pushing, and you will birth a miracle.

Most Christians have this idea that all you have to do is get saved and everything will be turned around in an instant. Well, in one sense, that's true. In God's eyes, you are created new, and everything you've ever done or has been done to you is erased. To him, your life is turned around instantaneously; however, for women who have been broken for a long time, the repair might be a lengthy process. Yes, salvation is easy; all it takes is a few words, but making the heart believe is harder. Trusting someone after being hurt isn't easy, and it does take time. If you're wondering why it's taking so long for you to come to Jesus, it's okay. Just don't quit coming. Take a step every day if you need to. He'd love it if we all just ran into his arms but some of us need to take baby steps and approach with caution.

God doesn't care how long it takes just as long as you keep stepping. Remember, he has your halo, and every step you take just gets you that much closer to what is rightfully yours. He's not going to toss it to you because you'll just lose it again. You have to come to the throne room of God to get it.

5

Grabbing Hold of Your Halo

Once you've realized that Jesus Christ is the only way to have your life back and you've come to the throne room to get it, you must accept Jesus Christ as your Lord and Savior. In order to do that, you must believe in your heart and confess with your mouth that Jesus Christ is Lord. You must truly believe and admit that he is the son of God who was raised from the dead for your sins. You must believe the gospel. There is no other way to get saved, no matter what others may tell you. That is the first step, but don't stop there. Many people get hold of that concept but don't go any further, and they never get their halo back. They can view it, as Jesus still holds it, but they are missing a few key steps to getting it back. One of these steps is the forgiveness step. That's right; you must forgive yourself and the people who have hurt you before you can truly be the person God created you to be. Before you can wear your halo perfectly well, forgiveness is mandatory.

Forgiver of the Brethren

Knowing who the real robber is and that your only advocate is Jesus Christ shouldn't make you intimidated or scarred. Knowing what you're up against and knowing the truth simply gives you power. When you understand the scripture that says, "For we wrestle not against flesh and blood, but against principalities, against powers, against the rulers of the darkness of this world, against spiritual wickedness in high places" (Eph. 6:12, KJV), you become a better fighter. You become aware of his tactics, and thus, you can adopt a better strategy.

The best strategy of defense is not what the world tells you to do. In order to retrieve your halo, get your life back together, trust again, and feel joyful and hopeful again, you must do the one thing you don't want to do. You must forgive. The Bible calls us to forgive, pray for, and do good to those who use us and curse us. Your emotions may be telling you to do the exact opposite. You might feel like yelling at, getting even with, and causing pain to those who have used you, but that's not God's way. If God is the one who gave you your halo, then he can tell you how to get it back. You have to do it through forgiveness and love. I admit that forgiveness is one of the single hardest things you will ever do. Yet, if you can muster the courage and faith to forgive the person who has cut your heart so deeply, you will recover miraculously.

I thought I had truly forgiven those who had hurt me, but all I had really done was bury the hurt deep inside. I had become a master at masking emotions. I had convinced myself I was "over it." Yes, I was much too mature of a Christian to harbor feelings of pain, hurt, resentment, bitterness, or anger. When these feelings would arise, I'd think of something different, put on a worship song, or get busy doing something. I thought I was an expert at controlling emotions. While those tactics for coping are helpful and even appropriate, something has to happen first before they actually work. What I'm about to tell you is the very thing you don't want to hear. It's the very thing other people in your life don't want me to tell you. But it must be done. Once you accept Jesus Christ as your Savior, you must go to the deepest pit of pain you can imagine. You have to relive your past. You have to acknowledge all the dirty truths that you have been subjected to. You might need to say things out loud, you might need to write them down, or you might need to tell them to someone else. You might need to have one last, long cry. You may have to scream at the top of your lungs. I don't know what you might have to do, but you have to get it out in order to let it go. While writing this book, I had to relive my past hurts. I had to allow my rage at my father to burst forth. I had to go back to that night in the car by the riverbank. I had to tell myself that it was not okay for him to take whatever he wanted. I had to relive the physical assaults of my first husband and feel the agony of betrayal once again with my second marriage. I had to go to the deepest pit I could possibly take my soul to in order to face it. For me, it was a time period of confronting my nightmares. Just as Jesus had to endure the suffering on the cross in order to be resurrected, we must go through the same. He allowed himself to go through the pain knowing victory awaited him on the other side. Many times we go through the pain as well, but we don't acknowledge the cross. Many women bury the hurt quickly because they have too many obligations and child care duties to tarry at the cross. I'm not suggesting you stay in this place of misery and despair. However, if you sense that you are not able to let go of past hurts, you might need to face them one last time. But this time you can do it from the perspective of a victor, not a victim. Many people asked me why I had to write all the shameful secrets my life held. Why couldn't I just gloss over the details? The answer is this: In order to understand the depths of forgiveness and the breadth of God's love, you must go through the depths of your pain. You can only truly forgive someone when you understand just how deep the cuts have been. You have to inspect the wound to know how to property treat it. Jesus was able to go through the torture as a strong man, not a weak one, because he knew of the resurrection on the other side. Perhaps when you went through your pain, you weren't assured of your victory, so you didn't face the hurt well. But this time, if you will relive the past from a place of confidence and power, knowing you've come through it and will continue to be victorious from here on out, you will receive such power and true healing and forgiveness can be possible.

Jesus did this perfectly. He went through the torture of the crucifixion and was able to look at his captors and say, "Father, forgive them; for they know not what they do" (Luke 23:34, KJV). We can learn a lot about forgiveness through Jesus. He knows firsthand how pain and betrayal can feel. Judas, his disciple and friend, betrayed him for thirty pieces of silver, Peter, the one he relied upon to build the church, denied him during a time when he needed a friend more than ever. Those who once walked with him and talked with him scattered. The guards leading him to crucifixion spit on him, slapped him, punched him, pushed him, mocked him, and shoved thorns into his head. They whipped him, drove nails into his hands and feet, made a mocking sign to hang above his head, and then laughed and jeered while he hung ashamed and hurting. They had no reason to treat him in such a manner, and he had every right to be bitter. He would have been justified had he been angry and condemning. Yet he found a way to forgive them because he knew he was the stronger person. That's what God wants for his daughters: to know we are the stronger person in spite of those condemning us.

You and I can follow his lead and be set free from the pain, depression, and hurt in our lives as well. We can look at the person, or persons, whom have caused us misery and say, "Father, forgive them, they don't know what they're doing. They don't know they are deceived. They don't know they are being used. They don't understand they are being lied to and manipulated. They don't know they are lost and confused. They can't see the mind control games being played against them." When you do that, you release yourself from bondage. I've had some women say, "But if I forgive him, then he'll think he was right in doing what he did, and that would make me wrong." Please understand, forgiveness doesn't make him right. Forgiveness doesn't make you wrong. Forgiveness simply sets you free. Jesus said if we asked anything in his name, he would give it to us on one condition: forgive (Mark 11:25). If you've been praying for your life to turn around, then forgive. If you've been praying for joy or peace, then forgive. If you've been praying for your financial situation to improve, then forgive. If you've been praying for healing, then forgive. Forgiveness is the only way to receive the blessings God has waiting for you.

You may not want to forgive, and you may not feel like forgiving. The very thought of putting to rest your resentment may just turn your stomach. I know, I've been there. I understand everything you may be feeling. I've felt all those emotions as well. But I finally came to the realization that if I didn't forgive, I could never feel happy again. If I didn't forgive, I could never be the me I wanted to be. More importantly, if I didn't forgive, I could not be the mommy of faith and courage my children deserved. My worst nightmare was every mom's worst nightmare. I worried that something horrible might happen to my children. Once I began learning about the word of God, I put my children into God's hands to protect them. I never worried about them one bit after that point until the day my marriage fell apart and I felt anger rising up in my heart. I was so furious and hurt that I didn't want to even hear the word *forgive*, much less have to do it. I had been hurt enough. I was done casting forgiveness on people who could only cast stones. My husband knew what I had been through in my life. He should have been the one who knew better. After all, he was a Christian—or at least professed to be. How could he kick me down just when I was learning to stand up again? It is emotions like this that are justified and right. They leave you appalled, shocked, and indignant. Maybe you have felt that way or still do. You were right, and they were wrong. You are justified in your emotions, and you have every right to feel the way you do. And, by golly, the only way he'll receive your forgiveness is when pigs fly. I felt the exact same way. Well, God gave me a pig-flying moment. It occurred when I read the Scripture connecting answered prayers to forgiveness. Mark 11: 24-25, in the King James Version of the Bible, says this: "Therefore I say unto you, what things soever ye desire when ye pray, believe that ye receive them, and ye shall have them. And when ye stand praying, forgive if ye have ought against any; that your Father also which is in heaven may forgive you your trespasses." It is verses like this that I call spinach Scriptures and liver verses. They are hard to swallow and even harder to digest and do. I knew what I had to do. My inability to forgive was blocking my prosperity. It was keeping at bay my peace and joy. My hatred was causing sickness. More importantly, my unforgiving attitude was placing my sweet little children in jeopardy.

Guess what? The same is true for you. If you're harboring any unforgiveness in your heart, then everything you love and hold dear in your life is hanging by a thread, and the devil holds the scissors. I had to forgive, and you do too if you ever want to be free. When you do, you will have the boldness and confidence God will answer your prayers and keep safe those things and people you have committed to him.

Even though forgiveness is mandatory to retrieving your halo, don't confuse forgiveness with fellowship. To forgive someone doesn't mean you have to stay physically connected with them. You can forgive someone, yet walk away. You can pray for someone from a distance if you have to. To forgive doesn't mean you have to stay in the same situation and be a target for more abuse. All situations call for forgiveness, but not all call for a relationship. For example, I was able to forgive my abuser but not maintain a relationship. Sometimes, it depends on the thief. If they accept Christ, repent, and change their ways, you may be able to maintain a relationship. It may not be the same as it used to be. Being friends or acquaintances is okay. You may go from an intimate relationship to brothers and sisters in Christ. But other times, when people will not accept responsibility for their actions and refuse to change, then forgiveness without contact is the only alternative. I heard a saying once that says, "Your ex asking to stay friends after you break up is like kidnappers asking you to stay in touch after they let you go." Sometimes, the only way to forgive someone fully is to have some significant distance.

No matter how the situation may turn out. Christian women are called to forgive. Remember, forgiveness doesn't weaken you; it strengthens you. Forgiveness isn't for wimps; it's for those strong enough to get their halo back.

We've All Sinned

Lousy, lousy, lousy! Have you ever felt that way about yourself? I've done some stupid things in my life and have felt absolutely terrible about them. I've hurt people, I've sinned against God, I've gossiped, I've lied, and I've backstabbed. I could go on and on, but some things don't need to be shared. If you know what I'm talking about, good, then you're on your way to recovery. All people, at some point in time, have sinned. We've all been a creep, a jerk, or a witch in some situation or another. Many, though, will not admit their actions. While it can be hard to admit your faults to other people, at least be honest with yourself. As mentioned previously, many times, we are our own worst enemy and we toss our halos aside willingly. I've been to prisons to speak to women who have all thrown their halos away. But whether in a physical prison or not, if you've thrown your halo away and don't admit your participation in sin, you are in captivity. You are being bound by a false sense of security that what you did was justified or not a big deal. Without repentance, you'll never get your halo back. Worse than walking around hopeless and unfulfilled, though, is the very sure possibility of going to hell. Repentance is the only way to escape the prison you've locked yourself into.

To repent involves a few things. First, in order to repent, you must admit your sins, shortcomings, faults, or whatever else you choose to call them. This can be a very humbling experience for someone who feels they haven't done anything too bad. From counseling others, I've found that the worst sinner comes to repentance easier than the one who whitewashes their sin. The murderer, for example, knows he's sinned without a doubt. The drug dealer is convinced of his guilt immediately. Those who have lived a life of so-called morals may feel their judgmental attitude or occasional gossip doesn't call for repentance. However, the Bible warns that one sin is no greater than any other. All acts of rebellion, whether great or small in your eyes, are judged by the one who sets the standard: Jehovah God Almighty. And all call for repentance. Asking for forgiveness doesn't make you a horrible, wretched individual. It makes you human. I hate it when I hear people criticize someone for being a hypocrite. If that person repented and is trying to change their ways, they are not a hypocrite; they are part of the human race struggling as we all are. The hypocrite is the one pointing fingers and shaking heads at someone else's downfall, all the while committing their own sin and justifying it. Don't let that be you. Be quick to repent when you miss the mark. I personally have to repent every day. I mess up every single day and must go to the throne of grace to find sanctification. It's not that I try to mess up or don't care. I'm simply human and may find myself thinking negatively about someone that day or being rude or frustrated or complaining or doubtful. These are all sins in the eyes of the Father and require forgiveness. They may seem like minor shortcomings, but left untouched and unheeded, something as simple as worrying on a daily basis can be the cause of losing your halo. You were never created to worry, doubt, or fear. God commands people multiple times in the Bible to be of courage and be unafraid. Allowing the habit of worry can turn a person from a faith-filled warrior to a wimp. Thus, your halo is still missing because you are not the person God created.

The How-Tos of Repentance

Repentance is four parts. First, to repent means a realization of your sin. Second, it includes a deep sorrow of your actions. In this step, you are grieved in your heart because of what you've done. You see your actions as not only hurtful to someone else or yourself, but injurious to God. Third, repentance means to accept that God has completely and forever wiped out any memory of your sin. Others may still remember it and even throw it in your face occasionally, but God does not even recall a single detail of the incident or incidents. Your Father in heaven has amnesia when it comes to a repentant sinner's past. Finally, repentance means to go back to a higher place. Return to a place of righteous fellowship with God. See yourself as holy, pure, and blameless in the eyes of God. Make a determined effort to not sin again. These four steps can be repeated over and over and over again. It only takes a few seconds. For example, let's say you're in the store, and the clerk is snotty. Without thinking, you make a snide comment and walk away. Boom, you hear the voice of the Holy Spirit telling you that you shouldn't have been so hateful. Your spirit convicts you, and you start feeling like a louse. Immediately say, "God, I'm so sorry. Forgive me for acting nasty and help me not to do that again." Then put a guard over your mouth so that you stop yourself the next time. That's it. It's over. Repentance has been done and accepted. Now walk away and forget it, but keep a check on yourself so you don't continue to make the same mistake. But what if you do? What if the next day your frustration gets the better of you, and you pop off a comment to the gas station attendant because the gas price is too high? There's good news for you. It makes no difference how many times you have to repent. These four steps can be repeated twenty times a day if need be or only once a month. Repentance is always there as a way to get out of captivity. Don't give up if you feel like you mess up multiple times. If you repent every single time, pretty soon the act of repentance will be a watch over your mouth. Before too long, you might feel like saying something negative to someone, and you'll catch yourself. Your mind will say, *Better not say that or I'll have to repent again.* Repentance is the escape clause God gave us to live a life without condemnation and a self-check to remind us to act according to God's commands.

Throw It Aside

Whether you are the one who needs to forgive or the one who needs to be forgiven, one thing must occur. Lay the sin aside. Once you've made the decision to forgive, forget it. People say, "I'll forgive, but I'll never forget." They have no intention of forgiving. True forgiveness means to let go of the past, let go of the hurt, disengage yourself from it, and remove it from your memory. If you don't let it go, you'll never get your halo back. You'll never be complete, whole, hopeful, happy, or blessed if you cling to the memory of injury. You can't begin today if you won't let go of yesterday. The Bible says to lay aside those things which so easily

Jamie Cantrell

beset us (Heb. 12:1). Holding on to bitterness, anger, and resentment sets you back. You may be trying desperately to put your life together, and you may be making great strides to finding and wearing your halo. But every step you take will be offset by two in the negative direction. You'll find yourself farther and farther from your destination if you hold on to hatred. You cannot fill a vessel with new wine until you empty out the old. In other words, you can't take hold of a new life and a new mind-set if you won't let go of the old life with its old thoughts.

There is an excellent story in the Bible about casting away hurt. In the book of Mark, a blind man by the name of Bartimaeus emerges on the scene of Jesus's ministry. He is sitting beside a tree when he hears that Jesus, a man performing miracles, is passing by. He is so anxious to receive sight he begins to cry with a loud voice, "Jesus, thou son of David, have mercy on me" (Mark 10:38, KJV). Others walking with Jesus berate the man for his incessant wailing. They are no doubt telling him to hush. To others, Bartimaeus was unworthy, and his situation was beyond the point of a miracle. Persistently, Bartimaeus continues with his plea: "…Son of David, have mercy on me." Finally, Jesus's attention is caught by the beggar, and he calls the man to him. As those around inform Bartimaeus his presence is requested by the master, the blind beggar makes an immediate and critical decision. The Bible says he cast off his garment and went to Jesus and was healed immediately. The last part of that story is fascinating. In that day, the government issued special garments, or coats, to people who had a legitimate reason to beg. If you were lame, blind, or otherwise incapable of working, the government would allow you to beg for money by the roadside or the gate to a city. They would give the incapacitated individual a coat to wear, which signified to others they were a person in need and had a right to beg. It was an ancient form of welfare. This coat was important. A person issued such a coat could not lose it, or they would lose their ability to produce an income no matter how demeaning it might be. Yet when Bartimaeus was called upon by Christ, he threw off his beggar's garment and went to retrieve his miracle.

The garment in the above story can be symbolic of anything. It could be sickness, financial lack, depression, addiction, or anything else which has you in bondage. It could also signify an attitude of bitterness and unforgiveness. We are so much like Bartimaeus in some instances and so unlike him in others. Just like the beggar, we may be calling out from our position of helplessness, asking for mercy and hoping God will grant us grace. But unlike the blind man, when we are called to receive a miracle, we take all our baggage, negative attitudes, and distrust with us. Christ is calling today for you to come and receive your miracle. He has your halo, a life of perfection and abundance to trade for your garment of hurt, but you have to lay the latter aside to receive the former. Be like Bartimaeus. I'm sure this man said to himself, *Christ is calling. I'm not a beggar anymore. I'm not blind anymore. I don't need this garment anymore.* Throw off your hatred and resentment as well and come to Christ with the same attitude. *I'm not a sinner anymore. I'm not depressed anymore. I'm not harboring hatred, hurt, and resentment anymore.* Satan wants you forever attached to unforgiveness. He is telling you that unforgiveness is your security blanket, a form of protection so you won't get hurt again. He wants you shrouded in bitterness. He's telling you this attitude is a safe mantle to protect you from further injury. He's wrong. He's keeping you in a beggar's status. Throw off the deception and lies he's covering you with. Open your heart up to forgive, and come to Jesus to receive your miracle today.

In a similar story, Jesus heals a man by a pool called Bethesda. This pool was a magical place. It was said that angels would come to stir the waters once in a while, and when they did, the first person in the pool got healed. As a result, there were many infirmed people lying by this pool. Jesus walks by this area and sees a man who had been there thirty-eight years. The Bible says that Jesus knew this man had been there a long time, yet he says to him, "Wilt thou be made whole?" (John 5:6, KJV). The impotent man began making excuses, "I have no one to help me into the pool when the water is stirred. While I am trying to get in, someone else goes down ahead of me" (John 5:7, NIV). Jesus answered him with, "Rise, take up thy bed, and walk" (John

5:8, KJV). We are so much like the Bethesda man. We have been in our despicable state so long that we are comfortable there. Perhaps you're in a state of bitterness over the offense done to you. It has caused you to become hard-hearted, angry, self-absorbed, untrusting, critical, judgmental, sarcastic, depressed, whiny, crazy, or all of the above. Women are notorious for going from one emotion to another in 2.3 seconds. This is where labels such as *unstable* and *nuts* come from. Good news, ladies: You are not unstable or nuts; you have just lost your halo, and you can get it back. However, to do that, you must take a good introspective look and ask yourself the same question Jesus asked the infirm man: "Do you want to be whole?" Many people really don't want to be well. The myriad of emotions they portray has become a habit. Perhaps playing the part of a victim is one you're accustomed to. After all, it gives you an excuse to go off the deep end every now and then. Perhaps you, like this man, blame everyone else for the reason you are down and out. There was no one to help him get in the pool. Maybe your family has all run out on you, and the one person who was supposed to always stay by your side left you at the side of the pool. I believe that many times people come into our lives with godly advice to help us, but we are so angry at the person who damaged us that we believe it is their responsibility to come back and pick us up and put us into the pool so we can receive our healing. Guess what? That man is not coming back to help you do anything. If he does come back, he is going to sit there and watch as you struggle on your own. Is it fair? No! None of what you have been through is fair, but the devil doesn't play fair, and remember, he is the one you are fighting. Don't wait around for some person or another religion or circumstance to give you your life back. Jesus didn't accept excuses from the man at the pool, and he won't accept them from you either. He simply says to you, "Rise, take up your bed, and walk." In other words, "Stop acting like a victim, clean up the mess that you're in, and get out of this place of despair." It is unfortunate that other people can leave a tornado wreck in your life and you are the one who has to clean it up. Yet God will give you the strength to do it. For example, I know many women who have had to watch their spouse walk away happily in the arms of another woman while they were left with the children and all the bills. The amount of responsibility that comes with that is almost unbearable. You may feel just like laying down in the mess of it and wailing like the man at the pool. Don't give up. Jesus is walking in your chaos right now and calling you to rise. Rise above the pain. Rise above the abuse. Rise above the insecurities. Rise above the lies. Walk with your head held high. You may be carrying a bed of enormous weight, but Jesus walks with you through it all. He has said that he will not allow us to carry more than we can bear. The real tragedy isn't in watching a woman carry the load placed on her; it is seeing her lying by the pool refusing to rise. Women may have to carry loads never intended for her to carry, but once you get up and begin walking, God meets you and says, "Come unto me, all ye that labor and are heavy laden, and I will give you rest" (Matt. 11:28, KJV). Jesus comes along to carry the load if we will only get up and give it to him.

6

Who Holds Your Halo

Once forgiveness is given and accepted, relief usually follows. Relief that you are not bound by any limits any more. Forgiveness, whether deserved or not, always sets you free. The sky's the limit, and you can fly as high as your faith can take you. No one and no attitude has hold of you. There is nothing weighing you down; all strings have been cut, and you are now free to soar to higher heights. This has always been God's desire for you. He says in Isaiah 40:31 that you shall mount up with wings as eagles.

Sometimes, it can be scary soaring alone, but have no fear; the one who holds the wind in his hand is there. He is holding your halo, waiting for you to put it on. Many men hold out an engagement ring, but Christ holds your halo, which is a million times more valuable and a billion times more of a commitment. Whether you are married, single, separated, or divorced, there is a man who desires to be your mate. Jesus Christ is calling every woman to enter into a spiritual marriage with him. Now, if you are someone who has been in a bad marriage, the last thing you may want is to repeat marriage vows. I had a hard time seeing Christ as my husband or God as my father. Husbands and dads have done nothing but abandon, lie, cheat, and abuse in my experience, so seeing God in either of these two roles was really hard for me. But I would look at other people, and their marriages seemed so solid and sure. I wanted what they had. But this marriage to Christ is better than any earthly marriage. It is a covenanted marriage, meaning there is a strong, blood-bound promise of protection, love, and commitment that will never be broken. This marriage enables you to enter into other relationships if you choose and still feel protected. When you are married to Jesus Christ, you have the wisdom, courage, and faith to make correct decisions about others. He will guide you into and guide you away from relationships that are helpful or harmful. He is the spouse that has your best interest at heart at all times.

In order for you to accept his proposal and grab hold of your halo, you need to know what kind of a person he truly is. So many times women enter into relationships with false information. I know I have been blinded from a man's true character only to find out later who the real person was. Men have lied to me about their addictions, past, likes and dislikes, financial status, friends, and more just to win my affection and trust. Perhaps you too have been deceived in a relationship. Well, with Jesus, there are no surprises. He is not going to tell you that he is a hard worker and then, once married, quit work and lay on the sofa drinking beer and eating chips while you make the living. Jesus is a straight shooter. What he says in his word is what you'll get in your life. In this chapter, the qualities of Jesus Christ are revealed.

Dream Guy

So who exactly is this perfect spouse? Who are you standing at the altar with? Who is it that desires to enter your home, your life, and your family? Will he be a good father to your children? Will he put up with your parents? Will he understand your mood swings, hissy fits, shopping splurges, and breakdowns? Will he treat you with respect, pay the bills, do the laundry, and fix the car? Does he cook, sweep, dust, and grocery shop? Does he take the kids to soccer, help with their homework, and go to church? And does he do it all with a smile on his face? The answer is yes, yes, and yes. Jesus does, of course, expect you to help, but he will assist you in whatever you need. He will go out of his way to ensure that the grocery shopping goes smoothly, the kids are taken care of, and the car runs without a hitch. If this sounds like a dream guy or a fairy-tale prince, then I guess you're right, with one exception: he's real.

If you want to know everything about your knight in shining armor, all you have to do is read his love letter. Your groom has written you pages and pages full of promises, undying devotion, and love. It's all contained in one book called the Bible. I know it may seem long, and it may take you a lifetime to read it, but it details exactly what kind of a spouse Jesus will be to you.

Trash Man

I don't know about you, but it seems like we grow trash at our house. I can empty the trash cans in the morning, and they can be full by nighttime. My husband has accused me of bringing home trash from work just so he has more to carry out. While my spouse is great at hauling out the actual garbage bags full of spaghetti cans, paper plates, and tissues, my heavenly spouse takes out the emotional garbage in my life. He hauls out the bitterness, strife, jealousy, and anger. His words speak to my spirit and heart and encourage me to let go of these issues. As I release this negative junk, he takes it far away and burns it so that it never tries to clutter my heart again. He also takes the old sins and guilt that you may be carrying. He bags your shameful past and takes it to the burn barrel. Gasoline is poured over the contents, and Jesus lights a match and tosses it in. With a scorching flame, Jesus watches over it to make sure nothing flies out, but that every scrap is turned into ashes, and the smoke has been carried away. This amazing man also takes out the inclination to gossip, complain, and murmur. The more I get to know my Jesus, the more he stops me before negative words can come out. When I'm tempted to whine and gripe, he captures those words, bags them up, and out they go. When I'm tempted to gossip about someone, he catches the sentences before they are released and rushes out the door and to the dumpster. Don't get me wrong, I'm not perfect, and there are times I still have a pity party or gossip session, but they are becoming fewer and fewer as I allow my spouse to empty the trash on a daily basis. Jesus is perfect because we are not. And he has called us to be perfect so he can have a spouse without spot or wrinkle just as he is. If you allow Christ to continually take out the trash, you will be transformed into a new person with no garbage pilling up.

Mr. Fix-It

Along with being the garbage man, Jesus is an excellent handyman. After all, his first occupation was that of a carpenter. What a perfect analogy! Jesus not only fixes things, he builds things. He'll fix anything in your life that's broken. Just bring all broken pieces to Jesus, and he'll mend each and every one. Just like your halo, Jesus will fix a broken heart, an oppressed spirit, a mind of fear, and your car, if need be. For example, I had a van with automatic opening doors. While we were traveling down the highway at sixty-five miles per hour, the backseat passenger van would automatically open. Needless to say, this is a surprise to anyone sitting in that seat. Of course, I encouraged all riders to buckle up and lean toward the center of the van. With the warranty out, no money to take it in for repairs, and a natural spouse not good with electronic vehicles, I was tempted to be in despair over this problem. However, I was not without assistance. I had the best repairman in the world. He made every atom in the universe; therefore, he can certainly fix a whacked-out car door. All I did was ask Jesus to fix it and then rested in the fact that I knew he would because the safety of his wife and children are utmost in his mind. Praise the Lord, the van has never opened while driving again. My natural spouse is excellent at fixing things also, but we both know it's because he has God as his partner. During a major ice storm one winter, we woke to find out we had no heat, and the furnace was making a funny noise. He claimed to know nothing about these types of units, but it didn't really matter because the second I knew of the problem, I asked Jesus for his fix-it skills. He guided Tim to the source of the problem, and within ten minutes, heat was up and running again on that five-degree morning.

A heart repair is no different for God. After my grandfather passed away, I was so bitter at God for letting him die that I distanced myself from him. I couldn't understand why he would allow him to suffer and then take him away when he was the only father I had for many years growing up. I had a broken heart and broken faith. Yet Jesus revealed his truth to me. He wasn't the one who hurt my grandpa, the devil was. Jesus was the one who finally delivered him from pain. Sometimes we get weary in the fight, and God allows us to go home. He was actually honoring our prayers by allowing us to fight in faith, and when we became tired and weak, he intervened and took the torment and torture out of Satan's hands and gave rest to my grandfather and to the rest of us.

During my divorce, my heart was wounded with a deadly force, but again, Jesus picked up all the pieces and filled the hole left by the devil's darting arrow. He comforted me and gave me renewed hope and strength. I don't really know how he did it. All I know is that I would cry myself to sleep but wake in the morning with a peace that passes all understanding. If he can perform heart surgery in the middle of the night for me, he can do it for you too. All you have to do is accept his proposal.

The body too is within Jesus's scope of improvements. Healing is a promise he makes to you when you become his wife. There are a multitude of Scriptures that portray Jesus as the healer. He healed lepers, lame people, blind and deaf individuals, those with every disease imaginable, and he even brought the dead back to life. As a living testimony, I've been diagnosed with some horrible diseases—one in particular was deadly—but I asked my loving spouse to heal me, and he did. You are married to the best surgeon in the world. God made every cell in your body. Every blood vessel, every bone, and every organ and tissue was made by his command. Surely he can fix a minor or major malfunction.

Whether it is a home-improvement project, automobile repair, physical defect, or a mending of the heart, Jesus Christ is fully capable of tackling the job with perfect results. His tool belt is full of miraculous powers, and he's never without it. As the *Bob the Builder* theme song so accurately asks, "Can he fix it?" "Yes he can!"

Best Friend

I know it doesn't seem like it can get any better, but it can. Who wouldn't want their spouse to be their best friend? I can honestly say that Jesus is my dearest and best friend. I have my mother to thank for making the introductions years ago when I was just a baby. She invited Jesus to come into our home and become acquainted with her children. Since then, he has been my most loyal friend. Even though I've neglected him, ignored him, and snubbed him a time, or two, or three in my life, he has always stayed faithful. Maybe you have done the same thing. The good news is he's always stayed true to the friendship. Jesus will never talk bad about you. He'll never pick on you, make fun of you, or criticize you. It doesn't matter if you are or ever have been the object of criticism by a man; Jesus has never and will never be guilty of such actions. In fact, he stands up for you when others put you down. It doesn't matter what you've done in your life or how low you've acted, he has always been your biggest advocate and true friend. He is the one you can tell your deepest, darkest secrets to, and he'll never reveal them to anyone. He is the friend that listens when your need someone to talk to. He is the one you can rant and rave to, and he quietly nods until you're through. He is the one you can shop with, eat chocolate with, and watch movies with. He is never too busy to talk to you or spend time with you.

The best part about being best friends with your spiritual spouse is that he is someone you can laugh with. Jesus has the most amazing personality and sense of humor. Some see him as stoic and unapproachable. They assume he is serious all the time and rarely amused. The fact is; Jesus is funny. We have shared many jokes and moments of hilarious outbursts. Sometimes I can be at work or walking through the store and I'll hear Jesus say, "Watch that" or "Look over there" or "Listen to those people." And it will be something that either makes me smile or almost fall over with uncontrollable laughter. When you begin to see this side of Jesus, your relationship with him can be a lot of fun.

Jesus told his disciples repeatedly of his joy. In John 15:11, Jesus says, "My joy might remain in you, and that your joy might be full (KJV)." Jesus is the biggest joyride you'll ever experience. He is patient, kind, never sarcastic, rude, or judgmental. Every negative comment others may make about you falls on deaf ears with him. He only builds you up and puts you on a pedestal because he is your best friend.

The Good Provider

In the 1950s a term was coined concerning men. Husbands were called *the good provider.* Of course, that title was only given to husbands who were actually good providers for their families. The term implied that the financial responsibility for making a good home lay with the man. The wife was not expected to work and could expect her husband to provide a good living for her and the children. Somehow, in our modern society, we have gotten away from that concept. Perhaps, due to women's liberation, women see the man's role of a provider as biased against them. Regardless of why the role has changed, it has, and we now see three different scenarios. First, both spouses are working either to make ends meet or out of obligation. Second, in some marriages, only one person is working, but he or she does so resentfully. Third, there is a growing number of families in which neither are working, or working very diligently, and are relying on the government to be their provider.

Of course there are other scenarios out there, but these are the most common. Of course, the Bible tells us to work and not be lazy, but what happens when you do that and there is still not enough money to meet the need? Just because you or your natural spouse may be falling short in the good provider role doesn't mean you have to live in lack. Your spiritual spouse is not only a good provider, he is a perfect provider. He has promised you, with his marriage vows, that he will meet all your needs according to his riches in glory (Phil. 4:19). Financial provision is a promise of being the bride of Jesus Christ. While many religious groups dispute this claim, it doesn't change the facts. Jesus has given me, you, and every other believer who enters into his marriage contract a promise of financial security. The Bible tells us that it has never seen the righteous forsaken or his seed begging bread (Ps. 37:25). It also tells says that he will make everything your hand touches to prosper (Deut. 15:10). You are told that your barns, your place of savings, shall overflow (Deut. 28). God tells you that he has given you power to get wealth (Deut. 8:18) and that he takes pleasure in the prosperity of his servants (Ps. 35:27).

Don't listen to others who try to tell you that Christians should be poor. Don't believe that your income or your spouse's income is all you've got as means of support. If you enter into a marriage with Jesus, you have just married a multimillionaire who is more than willing to share.

Fierce Protector

I know it doesn't seem like it can get any better, but it can and will. The man who is on bended knee asking for your hand is very protective. Not protective in a smothering, jealous kind of way, but protecting in a "big daddy bear" kind of way. In the Bible, God is referred to as our deliver, protector, stronghold, fortress, and high tower. He will protect you and deliver you from every demon, calamity, tragedy, or injury. Psalm 91 details the protection God has over those who trust in him. He promises to keep you safe in every situation. I've personally been delivered from a tornado, an attacker, car wrecks, and more. The Bible tells us that he takes hold together with us against our infirmities. Jesus is grabbing your hand and holding on for dear life to fight with you against any weakness, hurt, pain, addiction, demon, or calamity the devil tries to throw your way. He is fighting with you and for you.

I've learned to expect my fierce protecting spouse to come to my aid when I need him. He showed me just how present a source of help he is one night when I was home alone. We used to live in the country about a mile away from the nearest house. Our home was located on the brink of hundreds of acres of government land. There was a shooting range on this property as well as four wheeling trails. It was also a prime place for late-night parties and meth labs due to its isolated surroundings. When I lived there, I experienced several late-night visitors who were either drunk or stuck in the mud and in need of a phone. God instructed me as to who to open the door to and who not to. He saved my life, I'm sure, on many occasions. Living in such a strange place with potentially dangerous activity, I was naturally a little worried at times. I've never been a fearful person, but at times I would get the jitters. One night, when my two children were babies, I woke up with a fear gripping my heart that someone or something was outside trying to get in. My spouse was working away from home, and I was all alone in this tree-shrouded home with two small children. I lay in bed for a while, listening to the sound of creaks, cracks, and all sorts of imaginary sounds. My concern for my children won over the fear for my life, so I tiptoed into my son's room. He was right across the hall from me; he was sound asleep, and his room was secure. My three-year-old daughter, on the other hand, had recently been moved to a room down the hall. She was at the other end of the house where there were three outside doors, one leading out of her room and on to the front deck. With heart pounding and breath held, I crept past the dark game room, living room, and kitchen. I entered her bedroom and quickly knelt by her bed. She was snuggled under her Barbie covers, and everything was secure. I breathed a sigh of relief knowing that all was well. I was angry with myself for being so fearful. I knew the fear was just Satan's way of trying to terrorize me. I stayed kneeling and thanked God for keeping my children safe. As I rose, I glanced above her bed where a picture hung. It was a picture I had bought when she was born. The print showed a little child asleep in a bed with a mighty angel standing over. The angel was a massive man. He held a spear in one hand and a plume of fire in the other. The wings of this angel looked to be about six feet, and each was wrapped in a protective way around the bed. The intense face of the angel portrayed a look of fierce protection. I couldn't help but smile and feel a bit more comforted by this picture. But the thing I experienced next gave me more comfort than any piece of art ever could. As I turned to leave, I felt something, or someone, brush against my shoulder. A whiff of air, making my hair blow, passed by me as if someone had walked past. I glanced around the room again, noticing that the air was off, and no windows were opened anywhere in the house. Puzzled by this strange phenomenon, I continued walking out of the room and back down the hall. As I reached the living room, I heard a voice singing, "I can feel the brush of angel's wings, I see glory on each face; surely the presence of the Lord is in this place." I knew, at that moment, the angel I saw in my daughter's picture was in my home protecting me and my children from danger. I have never worried about my children since.

My son, Legend, is now seventeen and is a living testimony to God's protective angels. He has been in the emergency room over a dozen times in his teenage years. He has had six broken ribs, a broken ankle, three concussions, major burns to his face, eye ulcers, a twisted atlas in his neck, a separated breastplate, and multiple stitches from dirt bikes and bull rides. Not to mention all the bruises, scrapes, and cuts that didn't require hospital visits anymore. Unless it's major, we don't go to the doctor; we try to sew and glue him up ourselves. There is a running joke in our home now that whichever angel is delegated the job of protecting Legend that day must have drawn the short straw. We can laugh about the incidents because Legend likes to live life in a big way and take risks on a daily basis. That's just who he is. God loves this daredevil more than I could ever be capable of loving, and he sends his angels to the frontline to defend and protect him every day. I am confident that Jesus loves me so much that he is a fierce protector. He will personally come rescue me or send his mighty angels to keep me and my loved ones safe. He'll do the same for you. He loves your children more than you do, and you can place them into his protective care.

When you accept the Lord's proposal, be confident this is one man who will die for you. In fact, he already did. He allowed Satan to bruise him and crucify him all because of you. He has already proven his vow: "Till death do we part." The good thing is, because of his death, you shall never be parted from him again. You have a spouse who will defend you forever. He will move heaven and earth to rescue you every time you call.

Smooth Talker

Last but not least, unlike some men who can say all the right words, Jesus can say all the right words and mean them. This guy is one smooth talker. He will tell you you're beautiful, smart, funny, and wonderful. He will tell you over and over again that he loves you. John 3:16 should be enough proof. He spoke to you and told you that God so loved the world that he gave his only begotten son that whosoever should believe on him would have eternal life. In John 17: 20–23, Jesus prays that we understand that God loves us as much as he loved him. Every time I pray, I hear that sweet familiar voice that says, "I love you." Some men have trouble saying those three little words, and some say it and don't mean it; but not Jesus. He said it, he meant it, and he proved it. He loved you before you were born, he loved you when you were deep in sin, and he loved you when you turned your back on him. He loved you when you were unlovable, and he loves you now. He will love you forever. His Bible is one big love story to you. All creation was devised because God wanted someone to love. Every prophet who came on the scene confessed of the love of God. The crucifixion of Gods own son was a plan born out of love for you. He went to extreme measures to prove his selfless love. Jesus succumbed to torture because of love. He endured ridicule and scorn because of his love for you. He rose again because his love was one of undying devotion. He could not die because love can never fail, and he had to rise again to bring you into a place of acceptance, worth, value, redemption, and life. He allowed himself to be pierced with nails so that he could take your place. He took our punishment because he loved us. He rose again so that he could come live in our hearts through the Holy Spirit. Can you see how much the Father and Son desire to be one with every single person? What extreme measures they went through just to prove love. So when you hear the childhood song that sings, "Yes, Jesus loves me. Yes, Jesus loves me," those aren't just words being spouted. You indeed have one true love and a smooth talker that knows just what to say right when you need to hear it.

Jesus Christ is all of these things and more. Take his hand. Take your halo. Get ready to experience a new life. A journey of self-growth and tremendous grace.

7

Wear It Well

Now that you've accepted Christ as your Lord and Savior, you have forgiven yourself and others, and you know who Christ is to you, you are ready to put your halo back on. I've never worn a real halo before. It isn't like a crown. It doesn't have side combs to stick in your hair. There are no bobby pins to hold it on. It is a mysterious, celestial circle of light that floats above your head. At least that's what it appears to be when you look at pictures of angels wearing their halos. In my mind, it is a package of traits, talents, and gifts God has given to you. It is fitting that the visual representations we have of halos are floating above the head. I believe that these talents, gifts, and traits must be illuminated in the mind. Changing and transforming the mind is the toughest thing to do. But Christ calls us to renew our minds daily with the word of God (Rom. 12:2).

Drop the Attitude

To renew your mind daily, you must concentrate and meditate on the word of God. You must read the Bible, listen to godly teaching, and make the transformations you find in there. It is a process of dropping your own ideas and adopting God's.

Many hurt women adopt an attitude when they've gone through something painful. These attitudes can run the spectrum from defensive, judgmental, and tough to those of being the victim, needy, and crazy. I hear women say, "But you don't know what I've been through," when they are corrected for their attitude or feelings. Yes, it's true, you may have been through some horrific things, but the world and other people will not move over for your sad life. The world will not give you a break. It was here first. You don't get special allowances because you've been hurt. I know that may sound harsh and uncaring, but it is the most honest and caring thing I can tell you. Once you've risen from the ashes, brush yourself off and be transformed into the woman of courage God created you to be.

Many people say, "I can't help how I feel." Yes, you can! You can absolutely control how you feel. Feel free to have emotions, but don't let emotions have you. Resist moods and feelings when they try to arise. If you renew your mind daily with God's word, he'll help you do it. He'll help you to squash those negative feelings every time they rise up.

We are not controlled by our emotions. Instead, we control them. Practice positive godly emotions daily. Adopt love, grace, compassion, and kindness. Also adopt strength, courage, and faith. I know these sets of emotions seem like they are two ends of a spectrum. On the one hand, you are to be humble servants, while on the other, you are to be brave and courageous. That is the beauty of how God created woman. We are to be all of these. Woman was made to be kind, gentle, compassionate, caring, nurturing, encouraging, and patient. She was also made to be tough, strong, wise, and fiercely protective. I think of a lioness. She plays with her cubs, gives them baths, hunts for food, brings it to the whole family (even the lion), and takes care of the pack. However, don't try to come into the pride and hurt a member of it. The lioness is the one who will tear you apart. She is constantly on watch for predators. She is more of a fighter than the lion. I am reminded of a scripture in the New Testament. Jesus told his disciples to be wise as serpents but innocent as doves (Matt. 10:16). The only way to truly wear your halo well is to drop whatever attitude you've adopted. Let go of whatever feelings you've allowed yourself to feel. Quit acting on emotions that are destructive. Adopt God's demeanor, the demeanor of a champion. Be the lioness he's created you to be.

Adopt Faith

Taking on traits of God's character is the only way to make it successfully in this life. To become like God should be our life's ambition. One of God's traits, and perhaps the most critical, is faith. Faith is believing without seeing. Faith is knowing without having sensory proof. Faith is being assured that what you hope for will come to pass. Faith is judging God faithful to keep his word and his promises. Faith is the catalyst for miracles. In my first book, *Victory Ladder: How to Move Your Mountain with Eight Steps*, I teach about how to have mountain-moving faith. It is sometimes difficult to have the faith of Jesus, but it is not impossible. He told us that we would do greater miracles than he did. It takes faith to believe that. When you begin reading the Bible and changing yourself into the image of God, the devil and other people will try everything to knock you back down. Your own feelings and emotions will come creeping in to knock you off track. Understand this: God will not move based on your emotions. God will not run to your rescue because you're sad. God will only move when met with faith. That's why faith is such a critical part of your halo package. When you were a little girl, you probably had high hopes, dreams, and an optimistic attitude. You thought the world was at your feet. That's faith. And somewhere along the way, when your halo was stolen, that faith was taken too. Well now is the time to get it back.

So what should you have faith in? Have faith in whatever the word of God says. Have faith in your blessed and bright future. Have faith in your ability to overcome and be a victor. The Bible says, "All things are possible to those who believe" (Mark 9:23, KJV). Decide today that you are a winner. You are in this game to win. My daughter played soccer from the time she was four until she graduated high school. She played on a competitive travel team, and we went all over the nation playing. Those games were extremely competitive. However, she had the attitude of winning. She never went into the game planning on losing. She played hard but fair. She needed breaks. It was exhausting. There was constant running, watching, being alert—but she did it all to win. Ladies, we are the same way. Life can be hard, but we'll play fair. No matter how dirty the other players may play, we'll keep our integrity intact and play the game God's way. We might need breaks because this game of life is exhausting. Sometimes it may seem like all you do is run; however, continue to be alert and watch for the devil. He'll try to steal from you, but you won't be taken off guard. He'll try to use others to drag you down. Don't listen to their negativity. Don't listen to their doubts. Refuse to let them tell you that your faith in God won't work. Your belief system is none of their business. Someone else's doubt doesn't change the word of God. When feelings of doubt and fear come around, say, "No, not this time!" You have your halo back, and you're playing on a winning team. Faith is your strategy; you came to win, and win you shall!

Faith allows you to have high hopes. It enables you to know that there is always an escape path from the trials and troubles that come your way. The Bible says, "No temptation has overtaken you except what is common to man. And God is faithful; he will not let you be tempted beyond what you can bear. But when you are tempted, he will also provide a way out so you can endure it" (1 Cor. 10:13, NIV). Did you hear that? There is a way out. You may have to endure some things. I don't know about you, but I can endure anything for a short period of time if I know thee is an escape path on the other side. Paul was a man who knew what he was talking about when he wrote that Scripture. He was imprisoned, shipwrecked, and stranded more than once. He could have listened to his captors, but he refused to. He listened only to God and was set free and delivered every single time. Faith should be your primary attitude at all times. It should be the one thing people notice about you. Your halo exudes faith. It's part of its chemical makeup As Psalms 46:5 says, "God is within her, she will not fail…" (NIV) Adopt a never-fail attitude today.

Spit Shine It up

Has your mom ever given you a spit bath? When I was little, my mom would grab my brother and me before we walked into the store and use spit to rub on our faces to remove all the cookie crumbs, dirt, Kool-Aid stains, and more. I don't know why it worked, but it did. The term *spit shine* means to give something one last look and perfect it. It means to give something an extra touch of clean. When we first get our halos back, we may have them on and are wearing them pretty well, but we can always give them a spit shine. I'm a firm believer than we can improve ourselves every single day. Walking with God is not something we learn to do once and then do it perfectly every day; rather, it is something we improve on daily. Walking well with our halo is a process. We become perfected the longer we do it. There are two types of spit we must use to shine our halo. They are words and obedience.

Words are critical in our walk with Christ and even more critical in adopting mountain-moving faith. Jesus said repeatedly that we shall have whatsoever we say (Mark 11:23). If you say you are weak, then you will be. If you say you are tired, you will be. If you say, "I can't take it anymore," then you can't. If you say, "These kids are driving me crazy," be prepared for a nervous breakdown. Do you get the picture? Your future resides in your words. People everywhere use words of doubt and fear. They say things like, "I'm worried this will happen" or "I'm afraid I'm coming down with something." They confess fear with sentences like, "I'm scarred to death." These are not words for a faith-filled woman of God who has her halo back. The Bible says, "Let the weak say, 'I am strong'" (Joel 3:10, KJV). It tells you to call things differently than they are. It says it this way, "… and calleth those things that be not, as though they are" (Rom. 4:17, KJV). In other words, call the things in your life that are not right as if they were right. For years my son went through a wild phase. I just kept confessing that he was born again and serving God. When symptoms try to tell my body that I'm sick, I refuse to accept it. I say, "Thank you, Lord. I am healed from the top of my head to the soles of my feet." When finances are dwindling, I confess, "I thank you, Lord, that you meet my needs according to your riches in glory, and you've given me the power to get wealth." Speak Scripture. Speak the promises of God. Speak faith. Begin to change your language to reveal the blessings of God. Start calling yourself healed, blessed, courageous, strong, worthy, prosperous, self-controlled, forgiver, and stable. Call yourself whatever you need. Call in those things which you need. You can do this by faith, and that is the spit shine that perfects your attitude.

The next type of spit shine you need is called *obedience*. Obedience simply means to obey the word of God. You have a choice to obey God or not. God has set before each of us a blessing and a curse. Which one will you choose? Deuteronomy 28 is very clear on the details of the blessing and the curse. It lists specifically those things that fall under the blessing and those which fall under the curse. Let me tell you, the blessing is the best option. However, the only way to get the blessing is to be obedient to God's words and his commandments. It's not enough to just read the Bible and know what it says. You have to do what it says. You can't just talk the talk and put a cross around your neck and a fish-shaped bumper sticker on your car and think you're a Christian. You have to walk the walk. There are all sorts of ways to be obedient, and there are all sorts of things to do to be obedient with. The Bible lists several things like eliminating gossip, overeating, lying, and more. However, sometimes, there are little things that the Bible doesn't specifically mention but that you just have this inner voice telling you about. For example, I have an inner voice that tells me to make eye contact with people I'm talking to and give them my undivided attention. The Bible doesn't specifically mention listening skills, but it does encourage us to do to others as we would want done to us. So, being obedient, not only in godly laws, but in godly advice, is the little extra shine your halo needs. It's these two things that make a difference in your walk of faith too. When your words line up with the word of God, the angels go to work to bring blessings into your path. When your obedience lines up with the word of God, he can act mightily on your behalf. These two things also make you a powerhouse in every area of your life. Other people will see you as a woman of integrity and faith. The character emanating from your halo speaks volumes to the world. You become an example that others want to follow. You become feared by the devil, and you become stronger, more confident, and joyful.

No Tilting

So, here you are hopefully, halo intact and walking like a queen. Yet there is one last piece of advice you need to keep it secure. When the halo begins to tip, you must straighten it back up. Don't let the tip cause it to slip. Tilting of the halo occurs when you get into condemnation and guilt. If you've accepted Jesus Christ as your Savior, then your sins are cast so far away from you that you'll never be able to locate them. The past hurts are so far removed from your life you can hardly remember them anymore. Yet other people remember them. Others may recall your sin and throw it in your face. When this happens, don't let it tear you down. Refuse to be thrown under the bus again. You've been there once, and you've climbed out by holding on to God's hand. Refuse to go back there. There is an amazing story of a woman who was caught in the act of adultery. She was thrown at Jesus's feet for him to condemn and declare a sentence of stoning. He simply said, "He who is without sin among you, let him be the first to throw a stone at her." (John 8:7, NAS). One by one, her accusers left. He looked at Mary and said, "Woman, where are they? Has no one condemned you?" (John 8:10, NIV) When she answered, "No, Lord," (John 8:11 NIV) he said, "Neither do I, go and sin no more" (John 8:11, NLT). If Jesus didn't feel the need to condemn her, what right do others have to? They don't. God says that our righteousness is his business, and no one else has any right to say anything about that. He says, "If the Son therefore shall make you free, ye shall be free indeed" (John 8:36, KJV). Other people will want to keep you in bondage to your past, but God sets you loose. The world is full of judging, condemning, and accusing people. They enjoy throwing stones at those who have had a less-than-perfect past. God releases people from their past, but no one else wants to. When my husband and I got divorced, I was widely condemned for my decision. It has been a struggle to speak in churches. Some churches won't accept a woman preacher; throw two divorces on top of it, and you've got some serious stone-throwing possibilities. All those stones can cause a halo to tilt. But I have to remember that Jesus wasn't widely accepted by the religious folks either. He was threatened with stoning several times; yet he walked right through the middle of it and went on his merry way. We can learn so many valuable lessons from the stone-throwing story. First off, the stones from others might hurt for a while, but they can't harm us in the long run. Second, God is never the one throwing stones, and he's the one true judge. Third, people who have been the object of stones have more compassion for others in the same boat. Never throw stones at another. If you've ever been on the receiving end of hurling insults and accusations, you know what I mean. Hopefully, you've learned very quickly to never be on the throwing end. Lastly, stoned people have a lot to share. Those of us who have been through difficult times can tell others about the pitfalls and how to rise back up.

There is a story I heard once about a shipwrecked sailor. There was a man who was shipwrecked on an island. He'd been there for years. One day, he saw a beautiful yacht coming toward the island. As the ship got closer, the shipwrecked sailor ran out to warn the captain. Waving his arms wildly, he yelled at the captain, "Don't come any closer. There are rocks right beneath the surface of the water that will tear your boat apart. They are hard to see. Go around to the other side of the island and dock there." The captain, with his smug face and "I know better" attitude, yelled back, "Why would I listen to you? You're shipwrecked." Sometimes, shipwrecked people have a lot to share. Perhaps others should listen more to those who have been through difficult situations. Maybe they could learn how not to become shipwrecked. Even if others don't accept you for the transformed person you are, don't let your halo slip. Remember, you are wonderfully and fearfully made (Ps. 139:14). When stones begin flying, remember this: "She is clothed with strength and dignity, and she laughs without fear of the future" (Prov. 31:25, NLT). That is you!

Let Me See Your Halo

For all of you have made it this far on the journey to get your halo back, or for those of you who are still in search, I'd like to leave you with some bits of encouragement. I have been where you are. I may not have lived your exact life or felt your precise pain, but I know the ache that comes from being lost, afraid, used, betrayed, and confused. My heart aches for you in your struggle but wishes to rejoice with you in your victory.

Know that for every setback, God has a do-over. He has a wonderful life prepared for you. His word says that you cannot even fathom the plans he has for you (1 Cor. 2:9). He wishes to do exceedingly, abundantly, more than you can even ask or think (Eph. 3:20–21). God knows your past, and he knows your future. He has something amazing to offer you if you'll let him. So dream big, hope high, and never, ever, ever give up. Have a vision and hold onto it. The Bible says, "Where this is no vision, the people perish" (Prov. 29:18). Be a woman of vision, and never let go of it. It is yours. God gave it to you. It is not for anyone else to understand. Remember, "If God is for you, who can be against you?" (Rom. 8:31).

The devil will always come for a woman with her halo in place. There is a special fight between the devil and the woman. Through her body passes the future of the world. He will stop at nothing to make you stumble and fall. But no matter how many times you trip or how often the halo tips, you know how to straighten it up. Heaven forbid it gets ripped off and taken, but even if it does, you know the keeper of the halos. It won't take long to retrieve. Jesus will find it and keep it as many times as you may lose it. Don't ever think you've lost it so many times or it is so banged up that you'll never be able to contribute anything worthwhile to God's kingdom. He wants people with a past so they can use it as a platform for his purpose. You may be a broken ranger, but God has created you to be a triumphant warrior. There is a song by Dolly Parton, "Eagle When She Flies," that I dearly love. One of the verses speaks to a woman's fragileness and her ultimate courage:

> Gentle as the sweet magnolia
> Strong as steel, her faith and pride
> She's an everlasting shoulder
> She's the leaning post of life
> She hurts deep and when she weeps
> She's just as fragile as a child
> And she's a sparrow when she's broken
> But she's an eagle when she flies

I believe that most women have been a sparrow at some point in time. Perhaps you've been weak and fragile; now it's time to step into the role of an eagle. The past is nothing more than a story. It has no power to hurt you. The scars you've received are only a reminder of inevitable victory. Those with the deepest cuts have the potential for the strongest courage. God gave you a halo; he intends for you to wear it well. You have a divine right to take back what the devil has stolen. Pick yourself up, dust yourself off, and fight like you've never fought before. Look back at the past and smile, for the broken ranger is whole again.

CPSIA information can be obtained
at www.ICGtesting.com
Printed in the USA
BVOW06s2140171116
468244BV00008B/79/P